T0113807

The Ghosts of Ngaingah

Michael Fayia Kallon

Sierra Leonean Writers Series

The Ghosts of Ngaingah
Copyright © 2010 by Michael Fayia Kallon
www.makonabooks.com

ISBN: 978-9988-1-3983-4

First published 2010
Reprint 2013
This Edition: February 2015

Sierra Leonean Writers Series
c/o Mallam O. & J. Enterprises
120 Kissy Road, Freetown, Sierra Leone
Publisher: Prof. Osman Sankoh (Mallam O.)
publisher@sl-writers-series.org

Dedication

To Junior, Brenda, Edward, and little Zanaria: this book is another invitation to you to read about a wonderful group of people, the Kissi of Sierra Leone.

I also dedicate it to the memory of my late daughter Margaret, and to Prof. Osman Sankoh and the entire SLWS team who are doing wonderful work.

Preface

The Ghosts of Ngaingah is about a village on the west coast of Africa and a ritual curse that befell it. The Kissi have lived in that village since ancient times. Upon locating in the Kissi-Kama Chiefdom in the northeastern region of the Republic of Sierra Leone, they refused to follow ancient traditional practices. At the local oracle near the Kuyoh Mountain and at a shrine on the bank of Ndopie River, they heard a mysterious dirge one morning before the sun reached its zenith. The villagers saw a crowd of ghosts with bundles on their heads and accompanied by many animals. They were repeatedly chanting a mysterious dirge. The ghosts entered crevices in the Kuyoh Mountain and disappeared. The scratches they left on the hard rocks are still visible.

According to my mother, who was a young woman when the incident took place, it probably happened in the mid-1940s. This narrative, which contains humor, mischief, and magic, demonstrates how powerfully tradition and custom influenced the lives of the people of one ethnic group—the Kissi. The mystery of the singing ghosts still haunts them. I am telling this story so readers will know about one of the twentieth century's enduring mysteries.

Some names in this work are fictitious, excluding the famous paramount chief, Ansumana Jabba, alias "Memah" of the Kissi-Kama Chiefdom, who lived at Dia, and that of Chief Sombo, who actually lived in Ngaingah during that time. Nevertheless, what you are about to read is an eyewitness account of what occurred in that Kissi village.

Michael F. Kallon

New York City, September 20, 1997

Acknowledgements

I am glad to be the first to bring the Kissi way of life, traditions, and customs to the outside world. Such works cannot be realized without the assistance of one's family and good friends. In this regard, I am indebted first of all to my mother, whom I interviewed for this story. Had it not been for her great contribution, the mystery exposed in this work might never have come to light.

To my many sisters and brothers, and my numerous cousins, nieces, and family in the United States and back home in Sierra Leone, this work should demonstrate my diligence and stand as evidence that my memory of and love for my people, the Kissi, remain strong; the passing years have not eroded my identification with them and with Sierra Leone.

I am always indebted to the illustrious Burlington College in Vermont, USA, for their staunch support in my pursuit of a bachelor's degree.

A Kissi Song

A Bondo Society Graduation Day Song

1. In these times of ours
We shall sing to the young and old
On this graduation day of the Bondo Society
During this sunny, and dusty day of the dry season
We all come to sing, and dance, and to push them out

2. When no rains shall pour on our heads
Only clouds of dust may powder our faces
As these young women dance to the shakers
And the samba
And to the sweet songs of the Bondo god

3. Come, come, fathers and mothers
Come let's push them out
For we don't want to be blamed
For we don't want to be blamed
Come help push them out

4. These songs we sing are whispered by sparrows
The toucans hoot to their rhythms
And the toads and frogs echo to them
For these are the songs we and love-birds sing
And the young women shake their buttocks and dance

5. For when they are long gone to their loved ones
They shall see the significance of this day in their lives
It's the graduation day of the Bondo
Come, come, fathers and mothers
Come help us push them into their future

Kissi Version

1. N-ge dun –dah-Oh!
   N-ge dun-dah-oh!
   Yun-toh yan-loh-nah
   (Chorus) (Repeat)

2. Kalan-nchoire-vah nge-dun dah-oh
   Yun-toh yan loh-nah!

3. Paleh-wooh leng cho leng ni
   Yun-toh yan loh-nah!

4. Paleh-Bondo-leng mi sumuah-yah
   Yun-tooh yan loh-na

5. Yow-vah kendia mah solee chodun
   Yun-tooh yan loh-nah!
   (Repeat)

This song was composed by Queseo (Singer) Sia Ngeleh Foryoh, a renowned shaker player among the Kissi. She was also the author's maternal grandmother and lived in Yilandu and later in Koindu. Her parents originated from Denekendu, a village found in the Republic of Guinea, West Africa. This song follows the rhythms of modern disco-style music. Even today, it's still loved and sung by the Kissi during the Bondo exhibition days.

Kissi Proverbs

All Kissi songs were, and still are, accompanied by proverbs neatly inserted in witty sentences. They were probably the first to use the following proverbs:

"Little children can run, but they can never hide."

"A toad doesn't run for nothing during the day. Something must be chasing it."

"If a young man prepares some rice flour and boasts that it was prepared by his girlfriend; well, that is his own business."

"When a married woman comes to visit you, it isn't a good idea to accompany her home because her jealous husband could be looking out for her. If he sees you together, he will surely beat you mercilessly."

"The tongue and the teeth might fight, but it doesn't take long for them to be friends again."

"Those who sometimes get things don't need them, and those who need them don't get them."

"There is no bad bush in which to throw a bad child."

"A child that rushes to bathe in the river enjoys himself a lot before the crocodile catches him."

"Exposing your own secrets is just like smelling your own underpants."

"A monkey may sweat, but its fur hides the secret."

"Venturing to strange places sometimes bites but has no teeth."

'If a bird that doesn't eat rice follows those that eat rice, all of them will all end up eating the same rice."

"The goats of Kongonany are so clever; they do not eat the rice on the farms of Kongonany but go and eat the rice on distant farms and in distant villages."

"Anger against a child should only be felt in the flesh and not in the bone."

"A rabbit is cleverer than a donkey."

Chapter 1

Ngaingah and Its People

Before the northeast of Sierra Leone was blessed with motor roads just after Second World War, the Kissi were almost unknown in the country. However, they enjoyed a well-ordered, peaceful, and even prosperous existence—a people of culture and pride.

The Kissi believed in life after death and, as a result, named their children after famous forebears and visited shrines at the Ndopie River that runs near Ngaingah, and also oracles on the Kuyoh Mountain. They believed that the spirits of their ancestors lived there and would never allow evil to befall them and their villages.

One of their sacred rituals involved sacrificing domestic animals and cooking them, and then pounding softened grains of rice in mortars with long and heavy pestles until they were transformed into white flour. A few morsels of this flour was soaked in calabashes and formed into round balls which were then taken with the meat to the shrine at the Ndopie River and to the oracles on the Kuyoh Mountain.

On the bank of Ndopie River, the villagers neatly placed the morsels of food on half-submerged rocks, and then prayed, calling the names of their forefathers who were now considered their guiding spirits. They also prayed to God to ensure a bountiful harvest, to make their barren young women productive, or for general prosperity. This was how the Kissi lived. Even after most of them had embraced Christianity or Islam, they continued to pour libations at the shrines and oracles.

Ngaingah in those days was inhabited by people who performed wonderful deeds that awed their kinsmen from other villages who came to seek advice from the shrines and oracles. The prowess of the psychics and traditional and country doctors of Ngaingah made the Kissi-Kama Chiefdom renowned in the region.

The sacred activities in the village, its myths, and history were all the responsibility of their ruler at the time of these events, Chief Sombo. He always encouraged his subjects to give gifts to their neighbors and to feed the dead at the shrines at the Ndopie River and at the oracles on the Kuyoh Mountain. This practice is considered superstitious, according to the norms of Christianity and Islam, but what this story reveals could change perceptions about so-called superstitious beliefs.

All rivers are considered sacred by the Kissi, and the Ndopie blessed the villagers with so much fish during the fishing season that visitors to Ngaingah during the days of Chief Sombo were amazed to see such abundance. The women did a good deal of fishing in that river that contained a lot of river crabs, shrimp, and river snails, as well as fish. On bright sunny days during the dry season, the boys turned some broad spaces on the river into their swimming pool without much concern for the river snakes, black mambas, deadly scorpions, and poisonous insects that lay calmly on the river bank waiting to bite them. Such bites caused skin rashes and other skin diseases—all curable with medicinal herbs. The Ndopie River and its tributaries also provided all the water that the people of Ngaingah needed.

The Kissi carved cooking spoons from hardwood and surprisingly smelted iron which they discovered in rocks on hilltops or mountaintops. The rocks were collected and subjected to heat, and the end result was iron which they used to make hoes, machetes, and swords. Iron was also obtained from trading with kinsmen across the Makona River in Nongoa, Gbekedou, Tumandu, and Yendeh Millimo in French Guinea or in Foya Kama in Liberia.

The Kissi also made their own rubber sandals, but in spite of being so inventive, many loved to be barefoot, just as they preferred eating with their bare hands. That was how they enjoyed their food.

They grew all their own food—yams, peppers, okras, eggplants, and many more. They ate fresh foods daily and, so, heart disease was unknown among them. They ate cooked rice accompanied by different vegetables, such as cassava leaves, potato leaves, and eggplants, all prepared with palm oil and mixed with meat, fish, red hot peppers, and other edibles in the same pot with the African stock-cube called "Que-siohn" which was imported from French-Guinea. Que-siohn is eaten to this day in the Kissi-Kama Chiefdom. The cassava leaves were picked from the stems of the cassava plant and prepared for cooking by grinding them in a mortar and pestle; whereas potato leaves were cut by hand. They also loved okra, which was added to all the foods they ate.

There were no hospitals in the Kissi-Kama Chiefdom, only a small clinic that had been opened in the chiefdom headquarters at Dia. It was manned by physician assistants, who went from village to village curing the sick. These assistant doctors were highly respected by the Kissi, who sometimes considered them gods and gave them concubines, some of whom later became their wives. People with major illnesses were carried to Kailahun, the district headquarters, where there was a hospital. It still exists.

Among the domesticated animals in the village, the dog and the cat were most treasured. The cats chased rats in the ceilings of the mud huts. The dogs served as guards and slept outdoors. The dogs also assisted hunters during their hunting expeditions. They were trained to smell animal tracks. They could even smell where bush animals had hidden. That was in the past but not today.

Kissi villages located near Ngaingah included Kondoma, Njah, Yebeimah, Sarkpeh, Lepaeining, Mano Sewadu, and others. During the period of this story, these villages, just a few miles apart from each other, prospered and their inhabitants considered each other kinsmen. In the dry season, the villagers played and danced to the drums, the shakers, and other traditional musical instruments, such as the Kaelendon (Kissi) Balafon, which were played at every gathering. The drums, shakers, and the samba were their most sacred instruments. The samba in particular was believed to be so sacred that it was unwise to play it just for fun. Every beat could mean a prediction of good, as well as evil, for the player and even for spectators who only looked on and listened.

Dancing identified the Kissi as people of one culture. They danced to settle bush disputes and as a way of inviting the spirits of their dead to participate in cultural events. Afterward, the spirits returned to the distant land of the dead with jubilation, love, and peace. The Kissi loved and respected their elders. Whenever they joined in a dance, the women would take off their head-ties and use them to wipe the elderly dancers' faces. They would also wave the head-ties in front of them gently to create a cooling breeze. It was a sign of love, respect, and pride. The women cheered the elders until the dancing ended.

Those were glorious days in the Kissi chiefdoms. By working together, the Kissi enjoyed an abundance of food, harmony, and other benefits of a spirit of unity.

Chapter 2

Chief Sombo

Chief Sombo, ruler of the Ngaingah village in the 1940s, always sat in his courthouse dressed in a country-cloth gown with loose sleeves that resembled the leaves of a banana tree. He was tall, light-skinned, and very handsome. What made him rather mysterious was a single pigtail that stood in front of his head and curled down toward his forehead. He was an audacious hunter, as well as a farmer and historian, altogether a venerable elder in the Kissi-Kama Chiefdom. All the inhabitants of Ngaingah recognized his authority and respected his decisions. He ruled them so efficiently and fairly that his fame spread across the region like the wildfires that burn bushes in the harmattan.

His courthouse was a round mud hut built of sticks and many palm fronds. It had windows, allowing adequate ventilation, and was spacious with enough wooden stools, fork-like benches, and seats made out of raffia branches to hold everyone in Ngaingah. It was there that they decided their cases, organized marriage parties, and danced to the samba and the shakers. It was also there that they discussed bush disputes and shared farmland among the different households in the village. There also they decided if they needed assistance in reaping their crops, especially the rice that grew abundantly on the farms, and planned how to harvest the large acres.

Chief Sombo never raised his voice to anyone. He listened to all the villagers' problems and tried to solve them as fairly as he could. He had succeeded his late father, Sahr Sombo, who added laurels to the pride of the

Kissi in Ngaingah. The village had enjoyed great prosperity during his day, and his son followed in his footsteps. Ngaingah had prospered abundantly during Chief Sombo's rule and remained the most prosperous village in the chiefdom.

Chief Sombo was really loved by his people and kinsmen, and he returned their affection. He also loved little children and told them stories of the heroism of their ancestors who had fought the baboons, tigers, and lions that used to roam the countryside. The little children loved such stories, and they came in large numbers to sit silently in Chief Sombo's courthouse in the middle of the village, hoping that he would narrate his humorous and interesting stories and sing sweet songs to them. The children listened keenly as he taught them how ancient warriors were able to expand the boundaries of Ngaingah.

He was one of the most renowned snake charmers in the Kissi-Kama Chiefdom and could summon even a black mamba, one of the most deadly snakes, and hold it with his bare hands. He could also put a snake's head in his mouth and kept it there for a minute or two. He was always ready and able to cure snakebites. Chief Sombo was so successful in such exploits that he was considered, a psychic, even a deity.

As in most traditional households in Africa, the chief had many wives. Chief Sombo's head wife, Tuwoh Sombo, was of medium build, slim, and beautiful but shy. Tuwoh controlled all the domestic affairs of the chief's compound. In that polygamous situation, she decided who slept with their husband and for how many days or maybe weeks. This meant that her co-wives did everything in their power to please her, so that they could sleep with their husband. She played an active role during the farming season, supervising all the work done by the women and arranging accommodations for the laborers in the village. She expected the chief's other wives to be very respectful towards her or else, as a punishment for their rudeness, she could deny them the chance of sleeping with the chief for as many weeks as she pleased. She insisted on cordial relationships among all of them which led to productive work on the chief's farms. As the head of the village chief's household, Tuwoh also went from hut to hut to settle trivial family disputes. It was only when these disputes went out of control that they reached Chief Sombo's courthouse.

Chief Sombo was relaxing in his courthouse one day, enjoying the palm birds, lovebirds, and sparrows which sang sweetly in the mass of orange, mango, guava, pawpaw, and kola nut trees that stood in the village and on its outskirts. The chief was lying comfortably sideways in a hammock and smoking his pipe, which sent huge clouds of smoke towards the ceiling. Whenever he removed the pipe from his mouth, he spat many times on the bare floor as if abiding by the norms of some sort of Muslim fast. Afterwards, he would continue puffing away. The thatched ceiling was blackened by the smoke from the tobacco he burned inside his pipe. He never enjoyed this relaxation when his council of elders joined him which was often. It was on one such visit that they came to discuss the sudden death of Korfeh's wife, Tewah Korfeh.

Chapter 3

Welcoming the Elders

When this event took place, Chief Sombo was on excellent terms with Ansumana Jabba, paramount chief of the Kissi-Kama Chiefdom. Paramount Chief Ansumana Jabba was popularly known as "Memah," which meant superiority in a figurative Kissi expression. He too was loved by his subjects and enjoyed receiving gifts from them. These gifts usually took the form of sacks of cleaned rice, goats, cows, tins of oil, and even beautiful and charming concubines recommended to him as future wives. Paramount Chief Jabba attended most important events in the chiefdom, sad or otherwise, if they were brought to his attention.

In those days, whenever he visited any village, his presence and authority were announced by a village crier, a man who came outside early in the morning and went from hut to hut announcing at the top of his voice that the paramount chief would visit them on that day, and urging the people to clean the village and its outskirts carefully.

At the specific hour that the chief was due to arrive, someone in his entourage blew an elephant's tusk at intervals. The noisy 'boooo' sound was a clear indication that a supreme commander was entering the village. The blowing of the elephant tusk was followed by a wonderful display of traditional music played on such instruments as the samba and shakers. There were also dancers, and griots, considered comedians, who narrated amusing stories. Singing songs full of meaning and idiomatic Kissi expressions, they all processed behind the paramount chief as he lay comfortably in a hammock carried by strong porters. Those were the most interesting days in Kissi land, but they are now long gone.

This occasion was such a solemn one that, although he could not attend it, the paramount chief sent an emissary to represent him: Ketor, the chiefdom counselor. Ketor was a short, friendly, middle-aged man, well-versed in Kissi history not only in Sierra Leone but in Liberia and French Guinea. He was very proficient in interpreting Kissi traditional customs, especially on such an important occasion as the burial of 'a child of the river' and 'a child of the leaves.' He was accompanied by a group of elders with whom he could consult in case he needed assistance in interpreting a traditional procedure. They were all respectable men who worked with the paramount chief sincerely, responsibly, and energetically. They too were considered the paramount chief's eyes and were, therefore with Ketor, the most important men in Ngaingah that day. Their mission was to advise Chief Sombo and his council of elders on how to bury 'a child of the river' and 'child of the leaves,' according to tradition.

Ketor and his group were anxiously awaited in Ngaingah, for the paramount chief had sent a messenger ahead of them to inform Chief Sombo of their coming. He was a chiefdom police officer who had hurriedly come ahead of Ketor's delegation. In those days, colonial times in Sierra Leone, the chiefdom police officers wore short pants and tied a red cloth of a few yards long just above their buttocks. They also wore red hats. People called the chiefdom police officers "temuleh" police. "Temuleh" is a word used by both the Kissi and Mende in Sierra Leone to mean a length of cloth. The chiefdom police were mocked that way, because they tied a yard of cloth above their buttocks.

Ngaingah continued to be a highly congested, noisy place. The atmosphere was solemn in some quarters of the village but jovial around the shakers and drummers. Chief Sombo and his elders had already prepared accommodations and food for their very important visitors who arrived just after midnight. They were welcomed in Chief Sombo's courthouse and met the chief and his council of elders, the bereaved family, as well as visitors and sympathizers. They were given reserved wooden stools on which they leaned their backs. Ketor, the head of the delegation, lay comfortably in Chief Sombo's hammock. He had a pipe in his mouth and blew a few clouds of smoke towards the ceiling of the hut. He was given all the courtesy befitting his position as the paramount chief's private eyes in the Kissi-Kama Chiefdom.

Chief Sombo cleared his throat, held his pipe in his left hand, stood, and said: "Through you, Ketor, I would like to thank Paramount Chief Memah for sending you to educate us about the procedures that befit the burial of Tewah Korfeh who was not only a 'child of the river,' but also a 'child of the leaves.' It was indeed sad for me to report that Tewah died peacefully after a long illness. I would also like to inform you that the people of Ngaingah in these sad times have had a lot of cooperation and unflinching support from our relatives in the surrounding villages. They brought us enough gifts, especially enough gunpowder. We are blessed that with the wealth of experience in cultural matters that you have in the paramount chief's court, we can perform the necessary rites and conduct a successful ritual burial. Therefore, on behalf of myself and the people of Ngaingah, I would like to thank you for coming today by giving you the keys to our village."

He then presented Ketor with a few kola nuts in a small gourd. Kola nuts were some of the most useful nuts in the Kissi tradition. The Kissi not only ate them but also used them in many sacred rituals. They cured many illnesses by reciting incantations on the nuts, which come in different colors, the meanings of which are known only to the country doctors. Kola nuts were used as gifts and given to lovers to seal their vows. Hunters also used them as stimulants to keep them awake during their hunting expeditions.

Where Ketor lay, the elders of Ngaingah brought him fresh kegs of palm and bamboo wines. His entourage was also presented with the same wines. Since it was past midnight, the palm and bamboo wines were now sour and strong.

Yamba Farangoh, one of the most gifted griots and praise singers of his day, sat next to them in the courthouse. As Chief Sombo spoke, Yamba Farangoh emphasized the important points. When Chief Sombo called Paramount Chief Memah's name, Yamba Farangoh sang it out with Kissi idioms and proverbs, eulogizing the paramount chief as the 'elephant of Kissi-Kama.' He then kept quiet, as if he had not uttered a word. The praise singers were very important in those days. They acted as journalists, interpreters, and historians. They kept historic dates in their memories by counting the old farmlands that were cultivated after an incident had taken place in the past.

Yamba Farangoh eulogized Ketor, the chiefdom counselor, as the 'lion of Kissi-Kama' and then called for silence. Ketor continued to lie comfortably in the hammock, puffing his pipe. He sneezed and made a rude coughing noise, before clearing his throat and saying, "Chief Sombo, Chief Tengbeh, my bereaved brother

Korfeh, all the chiefs and elders in Ngaingah, and those that have come from the surrounding villages, I bring you greetings from Paramount Chief Memah, who sent me here today to help bury an important figure, Tewah Korfeh who happened to be a 'child of the river' and also a 'child of the leaves.' I know that Tewah was the daughter of the late Tungofulah and his wife Finda. She came from a family we consider to have some mystical powers with rivers. Because she was the only child of her parents, and in our culture the first child that dies is considered a 'child of the leaves,' as people of culture and pride, we have to follow the correct procedure in the burial rites. We are here to assist you in these burial rites, to sympathize with Ngaingah, and tell you that your servant, Paramount Chief Memah, thought seriously of coming but had important matters in his court. He is preparing to welcome the colonial district officer on a visit in the chiefdom. You know that the district officer is a white man who prefers to be toted by porters in a hammock like a bundle or an infant."

The elders chuckled and Yamba Farangoh yelled, praising the white man, and making a joke about a heavy human being carried all over the place like a sack of rice. The elders and even Ketor smiled.

Ketor continued, "During the days of Tewah Korfeh, everyone knew how productive she was. She cured most illnesses, and I will never forget how she cured Sakillah who fell from a palm tree and broke his back many years ago. She cured him mysteriously, and Sakillah was again able to climb the palm trees, having learned the lesson that it wasn't good to drink palm wine while up in palm tree."

Yamba Farangoh made the elders chuckle again by remarking that that bitter lesson was well learned by Sakillah.

"Thank you, Chief Sombo and your entire council of elders, for such a warm welcome and for allowing all of us to put our heads together so as to follow the correct procedure for burying 'a child of the river' who is also 'a child of the leaves' before evening today."

The onlookers gave him a round of applause and, still lying comfortably in the hammock, he lit his pipe again and continued puffing, coughing, chatting, and drinking.

Chief Sombo then invited his important visitors to go and see their lodgings, eat, and rest before the hectic ceremony that they had to complete that day. In every corner of the village, there was whispering about Paramount Chief Memah sending his most trusted emissary to grace Tewah's burial in Ngaingah. It showed the importance of the deceased, they said.

Chapter 4

Ngaingah in Mourning

The sun had concealed itself perfectly in the dark clouds and evening was fast approaching. Ngaingah was now even more congested, for relatives from Kondoma, Njah, Yebeima, and other distant villages had surged into the village in large numbers to mourn with their kinsmen. Some of the mourners had come to see history in the making as 'a child of the river' and 'a child of the leaves' was laid to rest.

These mourners were highly appreciated during sad times. Most of them went first to meet the chief and his council of elders to learn about the illness that led to the death of the deceased and about preparations for the burial. They were then respectfully led to their lodgings and fed, before returning to the courthouse or going to dance in the village. Some mourners brought gifts of cleaned rice, tins of palm oil, fowl, goats, sheep, and even small bags of kola nuts. Other mourners went first to the spot where the deceased died and cried their hearts out before going to the chief and elders to pay their respects.

On the eve of the burial of the 'child of the river,' Ngaingah was buzzing with traditional and cultural exhibitions and different forms of dance that added some humor and mischief to the occasion. The Bollah (distant relatives) made people laugh but in most of the huts, especially those nearest the corpse, cries of another kind were heard.

The elders had decided to present a cow, two goats, and fowl, along with bush animals killed by the hunters, to be cooked for the mourners. All of the domestic animals were soon collected, tied on sticks, and killed. Huge cooking pots were set on three big rocks, and fires were stoked beneath them by lighting dry bundles of wood. When the wood did not catch fire immediately, the cooks kindled the flames by blowing air or by using the large fans used to winnow pounded husk rice and dried coffee pods. From the palm trees on the dry land and bamboo trees in the swamps, many kegs of wine had been harvested. The wine was in abundance and flowing freely. Some mourners soon realized that the bamboo wine was stronger than the palm wine; it made them so drunk that they found themselves lying on the dusty or muddy ground in some corner of the village.

They also had the deadly cane juice, a locally distilled gin that burned the throat. Cane juice was distilled from sugarcane and had higher alcohol content than wine. It was found in the Kissi Chiefdoms of Sierra Leone, Liberia, and French Guinea. Cane juice produced in Liberia was exported to Sierra Leone and across the Makona River into Guinea, where producing it was a bit more difficult, due to regulations of the French colonial government. Illegally smuggling the liquor, cocoa, and coffee pods across the Makona River to Guinea was a dangerous activity then. Guinean soldiers shot and killed smugglers who did their illegal trade in wooden canoes.

That evening, the moon blessed the people in Ngaingah with such brilliance that one could have picked up a needle on the ground. The little children played "duduleng" (hide and seek), a game they loved. The palm wine tappers continued to supply a steady flow of bamboo and palm wines so that many drunken mourners lay in corners and in the remote parts of the village. The Kissi knew how to have a good time.

The elders ensconced in Chief Sombo's courthouse welcomed the visitors who had come from distant villages to sympathize. They were supplied with several kegs of wine and pints of the cane juice, as well as enough cooked rice and meat. At the courthouse, Chief Sombo narrated the history of Ngaingah and spoke about its heroes and the great deeds they had done. Each elder then told what he knew about the Kissi Chiefdom or his village. They joked, smiled, and smoked their pipes. They greeted the traffic of mourners by shaking their right hands in such a way that a sharp noise, like snapping, was audible some yards away. As a form of respect, the younger men and women greeted their elders by making curtsies and bowing their heads. They never used profane words in the presence of their elders. Any young man or woman caught using profane words in public was made to lie prostrate on the ground and given lashes on the buttocks with a rattan.

Ample gunpowder, supplied by the elders, hunters, and chiefs, was poured inside the barrels of their homemade muskets. The hunters then inserted a long stick or an iron rod into the ancient guns and tamped the gunpowder many times. After carefully setting the dangerous explosives, a flash of fire ignited the gun which made a loud noise that was heard miles away. The gun was fired many times during in the day to signify the death of a prominent figure in their chiefdom. This added respect and solemnity to the occasion.

Some of the mourners in attendance were famous musicians and comedians. After they met Chief Sombo and the elders, they played their traditional instruments in the village or performed at the chief's courthouse. Kongotibo was among the renowned praise singers always invited to grace such occasions. She came from

Sondokollorbendu village. Wango of Yegbadu village also came, among many others. Kongotibo and Wango had their own groups. They played the shakers creatively and also sang delightful songs. Supporting them was always a small band of singers and shaker players who inserted proverbs in the songs with their tuneful voices. They were all invited to Ngaingah to grace the important occasion of the burial of Korfeh's wife.

The renowned shaker players sang of historical events that occurred many years earlier in the Kissi Chiefdom. Although most of them are now dead, they are remembered for their mellifluous voices. Some still remembered in the Kissi Chiefdom are Yamba Farangoh, a griot who came from Farangoh village; Yamba Yilandu, also from Yilandu village; and Queseo (singer) Sia Ngeleh Foryoh from Koindu, an important Kissi business center and also the capital of the Kissi Chiefdom in Sierra Leone. There was also Kueyoh of Mendekorma village, located to this day on the Sierra Leone-Liberia border; Kon-ngee of Kpandoning village, still found across the border in Liberia; Queseo Kusedu of Kusedu village, just a mile from Koindu.

Another famous musician named Komeh was now in the village with his drummer boys. He lived in Buedu, the capital of the Kissi-Tongui Chiefdom. They came for the specific purpose of singing the songs of the dead during the burial ceremony. Tewah, during her day, had loved Komeh's songs and danced to them.

Kongotibo was well-respected and even considered a goddess of love, magic, and music. When she raised her voice in song, chills ran down the spines of her audience. Her songs were so moving that even Chief Sombo sometimes stood and danced, spreading his arms in his huge country-cloth gown like the leaves of a banana plant.

Some of the onlookers took off their head ties, wiped his sweaty face, and gently moved their hands in front of him to stir some air. Kongotibo's tuneful voice with its great depth and resonance rang with encomiums to the heroes who had died many years before and to those still alive. She mentioned Chief Sombo, calling him the 'lion, the eagle, and the dragon of Ngaingah.' The small group of backers echoed her so liltingly that the dancers and huge crowd of spectators were amazed. The humor of the singers brought fun and laughter to many as they danced.

Beaming, Chief Sombo said, "Ah! Kontogibo you are the goddess of our Kissi songs!" He loved to dance to the shakers and the samba and, with Yamba Farangoh by his side, followed the musicians as they went to every corner of the village, sometimes receiving gifts. The chief and his wife were a perfect match in their tradition, and Tuwoh Sombo joined in the dancing.

Wango was another wonderful musician. She played the shakers to perfection, eulogizing Chief Sombo as an 'elephant and a rhinoceros with a pigtail in the front of his head.' The dancers and onlookers giggled and raised their voices in unison, "Oh-Seah!" and concluded "eeh!" The mourners cried, danced, chatted, and giggled away the evening in the warm embrace of love and friendship.

Those, who had had some personal encounter with the Tewah Korfeh in the past, sat and cried non-stop. They knew that she was 'a child of the river' and 'a child of the leaves.' They knew that sacred items had to be put in the grave. These items were so sacred that no one, except the psychics, philosophers, and country doctors, knew what they were but, among them, gunpowder was visible among the sacred leaves put on the corpse before dirt was laid in the grave.

The young men in the village had been busy digging the grave that was just a stone's throw from Chief Sombo's courthouse. The little children weren't permitted to play nearby, because their parents feared that they might fall in by mistake and be injured, as it so happened sometimes.

As the moonlight continued to shine very brightly, the festivities in the village continued without interruption. Yamba Farangoh had a cow's tail in his hand and shook it sideways when he sang the praises of all those gathered there. He slept on a wooden stool and woke when he pleased or when the children, whom he loved, came to tease him. Children loved the griots so much that they brought them gifts, such as were mangoes, oranges, bananas, cucumbers, coconuts, and even kola nuts. The griots sang amusing songs for them; they would also ask them their names, eulogize the names, telling them that they were the heroes of the next generation.

Yamba Farangoh was offered a pint of cane juice, and he shook it as if in amazement, yelling, "Balika-tao-tao" (thank you so much). "Ah! Tamba-Nanjah" (Tamba draw me). He even uttered praises to the cane juice. Whenever a Kissi griot uttered any word, the elders and especially the little children laughed. Griots could silence huge crowds by yelling some eulogies, a technique they used brilliantly. The spectators would gaze at them, shake their heads, and laugh. Even when the griots ate, they never allowed any break in their performance. They ate and sang eulogies at the same time. Everyone enjoyed such antics.

Most mourners painted their faces with a sacred white chalk excavated from the swamp. The significance of the chalk was a mystery that only special philosophers, known as "sokoah" (Kissi philosophers), could explain. Only they could explain the local culture without any harm coming

28

to them through the invisible laws of nature. It was, however, believed that the sacred white chalk the psychics and philosophers used was a type of medium by which they could see into the future, perform mysterious deeds, and even see normally invisible things. The white powder had other mysterious powers known only to the 'sokoah' who were never allowed to divulge such secrets. One still sees this chalk on Kissi faces during important cultural occasions.

The flood of mourners into the village lasted until early morning, and the crying continued unabated amid the noise of the festivities. The moon had tried to close its eyes. The boys had made fires outdoors and roasted the beef they received as payment when the domestic animals were killed. The drummers used these fires to warm the faces of their drums, rested briefly, and rejoined the festivities.

The night was now long gone. A dancing site was chosen near Chief Sombo's court and close to the grave. Accompanied by a few singers, Komeh, the lead singer, and his drummers with four large drums assembled. The people formed a wide circle with an empty space in the middle for the dancers. The chiefs and elders formed the apex of the circle. As on any typical Kissi occasion, jealous men and women were concerned about whom their loved ones were chatting with.

The voices, the singers, and drumbeats echoed as far as Kuyoh, Njawee, Ngopie, and the Mambah Mountains. When Komeh sang, onlookers and dancers gazed at him with admiration and danced with agility. His voice pleased them greatly, for in resonance and style, it perfectly suited his songs that were full of Kissi idioms and historical and folkloric allusions. These gatherings made Chief Sombo famous. He was beautifully dressed and always danced by spreading his arms like a banana plant that had reached puberty. He was sometimes joined by other elders and that made the occasion grander.

When Ketor joined the dancing on this occasion, there were cheers, and the wiping of the faces continued as the drumming echoed all around. Yamba Farangoh sat in a corner, sipping his Tamba-Nanjah gin and giving out few "Ouh! Ouh!" yells in response to Komeh's eulogies. He never danced but only sat to eulogize all those who participated in the dancing on the bare, dry, and dusty ground.

Some of the elders were too old to participate in the dancing, so they sat beside the campfire and enjoyed drinking their palm and bamboo wines with a mixture if the "Tamba-Nanjah" gin. The drums echoed and re-echoed around the mountains. In Ngaingah, the singers sang soulful ballads and dirges for the deceased which pleased their audience so much that they responded with thunderous applause. Yamba Farangoh had a small talking drum under his arm. He was also a solo musician who played his talking drum with a short stick making sounds like the reggae and hip-hop rhythms of today.

How such musical styles emerged in western countries remains a mystery, for they are ancient Kissi styles. The sound of the samba was used to demonstrate sadness, courage, and the appropriateness of cultural traditions. The other drummers sweated profusely, while the agile dancers seemed to have no bones as they twirled and twisted. Some people lay on mats outdoors, enjoying the singing and the moonlight. They went to sleep right there, so that mourners from distant villages could sleep in their homes.

Having played their "duduleng" (the hide-and–seek game), danced, and eaten, the children had gone to bed long ago, so that they could enjoy the day's activities. Chief Sombo and some of the elders had also excused themselves to get a few hours of sleep. But the drummers were accustomed to sleepless nights. Yamba Farangoh had nowhere to sleep, so he sat down and closed his eyes. When the mourners and dancers teased him, he would wake up abruptly and yell, "Ouh! Ouh! Ouh! Ouh!" making them giggle.

Before daybreak, for a while, the drums were the only sounds heard in Ngaingah. Most parts of the village were now silent and seemed somehow deserted. Some of the drunken mourners lay with hangovers, while others sprawled among the goats, cows, pigs, and fowl that roamed freely in the village.

An owl hooted in the huge tree that stood on the outskirts of the village. To the Kissi, the sound was significant. Some said it meant that the spirit of the late Tewah Korfeh had sat on the tree and appreciated what Ngaingah was doing for her. Many nocturnal birds and animals added their sad cries to the hooting of the owl. Bush babies cried in the distant trees. Then cocks began to crow and the distant swamps grew thunderous with the choruses of frogs and toads. The noise increased the rising commotion in the village amid the samba, shakers, drums, and singers.

The young women ventured outdoors and rushed to the creek to fetch water, which they warmed, so their families and visitors could bathe. Afterward, they pounded husk rice and winnowed it. As they worked, they sang melodious folkloric ballads and sometimes the lullabies they used to comfort their babies and put them to sleep. One of those lullabies is sung to this day:

Kissi
Hae-yah o-koh
Ma-kia bengoon
Hae-yah o-koh
Ma-kia bengoon (Repeat)

English
Winnow on my back
And give me some grains
Winnow on my back
And give me some grains

As soon as the women began to sing, as if by magic, all kinds of birds appeared from every direction. They landed fearlessly on the ground and began to peck at the tiny grains that had escaped through little holes in the fans. It was a beautiful sight, seeing the birds hopping around and nodding their heads in time with the rhythm of the lullaby.

Chapter 5

Preparations for Tewah Korfeh's Burial

Very early, Chief Sombo led a group of elders to a sacred shrine near the Ndopie River to pour libation to the gods so they would accept the soul of Tewah Korfeh, this 'child of the river.' As usual, they also had collected a few white and red kola nuts, morsels of cooked rice flour, and cooked chicken meal to feed the dead.

At the site, Chief Sombo stood tall and, looking absolutely confident, said, "To the God of our great grandfathers, the God of the Ndopie River, and to all our forebears who have died and are long gone: We are here today to remember all of you. We are here today to feed you once again. We pray that you continue to bring prosperity into our lives, to Ngaingah, and to all the other villages where our kinsmen live. We pray that you will crown our farming season with a bountiful harvest. Your daughter, Tewah Korfeh, who also happens to be 'a child of the river,' lies dead in Ngaingah. We have brought you these gifts so that her soul may rest in peace."

"Ameee-nah!" (Amen in Kissi) was repeated after every sentence Chief Sombo uttered in his tedious prayer. He then took a piece of each food item they had brought and laid it on the half-submerged rocks, murmuring an incantation. Again, the onlookers repeated in unison, "Ameee-nah!" They then joked about the ancient men who had died and would never be forgotten because of their mysterious deeds in Ngaingah.

In the hut where Taweh Korfeh used to live, her immediate family, relatives, and friends had slept near her body. Chief Sombo, Ketor, and the elders had gone earlier to request that the corpse be brought to lie in state in the courthouse. Strong men came and took it there, having respectfully laid it on a stretcher built of sticks. When Chief Sombo and the elders returned, they held an impromptu meeting, the precursor of the long ceremony that would solemnize the funeral. Ketor, who was representing the paramount chief, was now the most senior chief in their midst and therefore presided over the meeting.

"Chief Sombo," Ketor called the chief politely.

"Eh! Massar (Chief)," Chief Sombo politely answered.

"Hmm, we have reached the crossroad of starting this burial ceremony, and I would like to ask if you know where the hunters can pick the "choire-e-pae-yah" leaves.

"Um-hum! Massar. Tungufullah, one of our trusted hunters, has already found the leaves on the outskirts of the village. We can get them when we are ready, massar."

"Okay. What about the calabashes, kola nuts, and other sacred items that will be used in the grave?"

"Massar, here they are."

The kola nuts had been neatly placed in a big 'yalantala' (calabash).

"Well," Ketor continued, "I was sent by Paramount Memah to aid in these rituals. I am now officially asking why we are here today, Chief Sombo."

Chief Sombo cleared his throat and said, "Massar Ketor, Tengbeh is handling these affairs in Ngaingah, and I am going to ask him officially to assume his responsibilities as of now. He is spokesman for Ngaingah."

"Thank you, Chief Sombo," Ketor responded.

"Tengbeh, the floor is now yours," Chief Sombo said.

Tengbeh cleared his throat and said in a charming voice, "Chief Sombo, the day for us to show Kissi-Kama that we are people of culture has come. I am also pleased to welcome Ketor, one of our venerable chiefdom counselors and his entourage to Ngaingah. Well, Chief Ketor, Tewah Korfeh is dead. She didn't die of snakebite nor did anyone bewitch her. She died of natural causes in her sleep. If you ask why we are here today, Chief Ketor, this is the main reason."

"Balika-tao-tao, Massar Tengbeh (Thank you so much)," Chief Ketor said. "Well, Chief Tengbeh, do we know the exact location of the 'choire-e-pae-yah leaves?" Ketor asked again.

"Yes, Chief Ketor," answered Massar Tengbeh.

"Then let us go and pick the leaves at once, since the sun is rising," Chief Ketor said, addressing all the elders.

They called Tungofullah and the other hunters to lead them to the place where they could pick the sacred leaves for the burial later in the day. The drums echoed and the singers changed the timbre of their lyric voices, to which the dancers moved energetically. The elders then led a procession carrying the calabashes in which they were going to place the leaves. The guns echoed and the dancing and crying continued unabated.

Directed by Tungofullah, Chief Sombo led the procession to a bank of the Ndopie where the leaves were to be found. As they walked quietly along the dusty footpath, the chief teased Tungofullah, saying, "Even a fly can't pass between Tungofullah and his wife Sia," which made the elders chuckle.

Tungofullah was the most jealous man in Ngaingah. He had a charming concubine called Sia, a beauty and therefore chased by the young men who lived in Ngaingah. Some even came from distant villages to try and get her. Tungofullah never allowed Sia to go to places alone. He was always watching from a distance, even when she went to fetch water at the creek near the Ndopie River. He sometimes hid behind bushes like a hunter and, if he found any man chatting with her, he appeared abruptly and told him never again to chat with his wife. Even on the farms, he was always beside her. Everyone knew that.

Chief Sombo saw a tiny green mamba that lay coiled comfortably on the footpath. Taking it as a sign that Tewah's spirit was guiding them, he recited some special incantations over the snake which quietly disappeared. As they continued along the footpath, an owl hooted on a branch of a distant tree. They also knew the significance of that and nodded their heads, beaming at the antics of the monkeys and at the sweet songs of the birds that circled overhead or fluttered in the trees. If one of the elders had hit his left foot on a rock on the path, it would have been considered bad luck, and the burial ceremony would have been postponed to the following day.

When they reached the site, Chief Ketor was asked to bless the tree before they picked the 'choire-e-pae-yah' leaves. "Oh! God of our forefathers; God of Kuyoh, Mambah, Jawee; all our sacred mountains and rivers; God of our great-grandfathers, we have come before you today to pick these 'choire-e-pae-yah' leaves according to the custom you left with us which we have practiced for thousands of years. We are about to bury your daughter, Tewah, who was 'a child of the river' and 'a child of the leaves.' I pray that her soul may rest in peace."

"Ameee-nah!" all of them answered in unison.

Tungofullah was told to climb the tree and pick as many leaves as he could. They were put into the baskets and calabashes they had brought. When they had collected enough leaves, Chief Sombo recited a sacred incantation, patted the tree gently, and poured some gin under it, as if to thank it for so kindly providing the sacred leaves that were going to be used for the burial.

Chief Sombo then stood in front of the group and told them stories about the old heroes of Ngaingah and the Kissi-Kama Chiefdom. They broke kola nuts and shared them. This was to ask for renewal of life and for guidance from the spirits of their forebears, so they could properly administer the rituals befitting such a burial.

On their way back, Chief Sombo again saw a snake—a black mamba this time, but it passed swiftly ahead of them on the dusty footpath. They could see the tracks of its coils as it meandered into the scrub.

"Aha! Tewah's spirit has passed ahead of us," he said.

So far, Yamba Farangoh had been silent, because he was witnessing history—the burial of a 'child of the river' and a 'child of the leaves.' Now, as the procession of elders returned to the village, he looked into his huge country-cloth gown, took out a pint of cane juice, and sipped twice until his throat burned. He then cleared his throat and yelled a few eulogies to the chiefs and even to the 'choire-e-pae-yah' leaves. It made the chiefs chuckle, and Yamba Farangoh himself couldn't stop giggling.

The sun rose, as the elders returned to Chief Sombo's courthouse. The drums, sambas, and shakers clattered and the dancers moved with vigor. Once there, the elders were fed. Gin and palm and bamboo wines flowed, and the ceremony continued.

"Chief Tengbeh, you have made it possible for us to get the 'choire-e-par-yah' leaves. What about the bundles of kola nuts and gun powder?" Chief Ketor inquired.

"Chief Ketor, here are the items," Chief Tengbeh answered politely.

"Thank you, Chief Tengbeh," Chief Ketor replied.

Amid the thundering of the musical instruments, Chief Ketor stood up and calmed the entire situation by declaring: "We have now reached a critical stage."

Telling them to listen intently, he said, "Elders, before we commence any ceremonial discussions here today, I would like to ask anyone to whom Tewah owed anything during her lifetime to come forward, so the family can repay the debt and allow Tewah's spirit to enter the next world with jubilation."

Tewah was a gifted person who never depended on anyone for anything, so those who came forward were people who owed her something rather than the other way around. All debts were forgiven by Tewah's husband, Korfeh, and the ceremonies began. There were no hunting expeditions during such ceremonies in the Kissi Chiefdom, so the hunters were around to blast the cannons.

Just as the sun began reaching its apex, the mourners surged to the courthouse where the elders had recited unending incantations over the leaves and the other items to be put in the grave. Festivity and crying were going on in every corner of the village. Komeh and his drummers and the shaker players with their singers and backers now knew that they would have to play non-stop until the actual burial throughout the night and even the next day.

As the toads and frogs continued to join in the drumming and singing, the cooking was completed, and the mourners ate their food. Ketor stood up and informed Chief Tengbeh that it was time to perform the ceremony of the blood. Chief Tengbeh agreed. A goat and a sheep were brought, and the elders went to the graveside. Yamba Farangoh accompanied them. The elders stretched their hands in front of them, touched the animals, and prayed over them with sacred incantations. Tungofullah

38

was then ordered to slit the throat of the animals, and the blood was poured beside the grave.

Yamba Farangoh yelled, and then there was silence near the graveside although noise continued in the other parts of the village. The elders stood silently. After a careful recitation of their sacred incantations, and the slitting of the throats of the animals, kola nuts were poured in the grave, and the elders returned to the courthouse for awhile. The animals were taken to a sacred place where their carcasses were prepared as food.

Chief Ketor again asked the elders to go to the shrine of the Ndopie to pour fresh libation to the spirits of their forbears who they believed now lived in the rivers, the mountains, shrines, and the oracles. Yamba Farangoh yelled out some eulogies to Chief Ketor, calling him the man who knew best how to perform the Kissi rituals on these occasions.

The elders took along a calabash with the kola nuts and balls of rice flour that the women had prepared. Again, Chief Sombo led the way as special protection against any evils that might be lying on the dusty footpath. On their way, an animal—a black bush cat—swiftly crossed the path ahead of them.

"Did all of you see that?" Chief Sombo inquired.

"Yes, I saw it," said Chief Ketor.

"What was it?" asked Chief Tengbeh who was behind them.

"A black bush cat crossed our path. It's a sign of good luck," Chief Sombo said. They all were delighted that every part of the burial ceremony was going so well. Yamba Farangoh eulogized the late Tewah Korfeh as 'a boa constrictor in Kissi-Kama during her day.' The elders chuckled again.

On the banks of the Ndopie at the usual sacred site where they laid the items for the rituals, they slit the throats of two fowls and sprinkled their blood on the exposed parts of the rocks submerged in the swamp. They again recited the dirges of the dead and laid kola nuts and balls of rice flour. After answering "Ameee-nah!" many times, they left. As they returned to the Chief Sombo's courthouse, no one looked back at the ritual that had been performed or at the sacred items which had been left behind. That was the custom and they strongly adhered to it.

In the village, the dancing and crying continued. The elders had almost exhausted the items on the agenda of the burial ceremony. They sat and relaxed by eating and drinking palm and bamboo wine and the cane juice.

Chapter 6

Yamba Farangoh's Story

Yamba Farangoh entertained them with a story that revealed he was indeed a highly amusing and gifted griot, "Ah! Pusuh," he began. "He was a brave man who kept many wives. Yet, he was very unlucky because these women fought day and night. They couldn't arrive at a mutual understanding, and Pusuh, not being a man of peace, never sought compromise among them. They lived in Nyomodu village and the chief, Nyuma, was now tired of this uncompromising, noisy, and cantankerous family. The wives could agree on one day and fight on another. Yet, they had all agreed to be Pusuh's wives. He had paid dowries for all of them, and everyone knew that in Nyomodu.

"Pusuh then decided to make individual farms for his numerous wives, because they fought too many times on the large farm he had laid for the entire family in the past farming season. This was how they lived in that village."

Yamba Farangoh had finally succeeded in seizing the moment in the chief's court, and the elders listened to him attentively. They loved stories. Some onlookers and even little children had summoned others to the chief's court to listen to Yamba Farangoh's story.

He continued, "That was how Pusuh and his wives lived noisily in Nyomodu. Those women were great fighters. They fought like lions and tigers. They fought like elephants and boa constrictors. (It is possible that these animals lived in some Kissi who are also considered medicine men and women.)." He stopped again to sip few doses of the 'Tamba Nanjah' gin, cleared his burnt throat, yelled for silence, and then continued his story while the onlookers cheered for him.

"Then one peaceful day, Kemah, one of Pusuh's numerous wives asked her 'diomu-dooh,' (mate) Tuwoh to lend her 'fellor' (fan in Kissi), with which she was going to winnow some grains of rice on her farm. Tuwoh agreed and Kemah went to the farm.

She had a wonderful day on the farm, but at dusk, heavy winds started, and rain poured down. Kemah then took her mate's fan to protect her head and started for home. She came to the Dakah River across which lay a heavy log bridge that villagers used to cross over the water to their farms. Kemah slipped on the bridge and as she tried to regain her balance, the fan fell into the river. Since she couldn't swim, Kemah couldn't retrieve it and, besides, the river had some very swift currents that could have killed her if she tried to rescue the fan. She went home and told her mate about the accident.

"Tuwoh had never had children. Kemah, on the other hand had beautiful children by Pusuh. This made Tuwoh angry and jealous. In her usual mood, she told Kemah that she should go back to river and retrieve her fan, no matter what the circumstances. Kemah pleaded with her, saying she couldn't swim and promising to provide her with another fan. Tuwoh refused. The case reached Pusuh He tried to reconcile them, but Tuwoh still refused and again told Kemah to go to the river and retrieve her fan, which was an impossible task.

"The case then reached Chief Nyuma, who also tried to pacify Tuwoh, but she had a different intention and refused even the chief's offer. She insisted that her mate, Kemah, should jump into the river to retrieve her fan. Everyone said that the fan would no longer be in good condition; getting another fan was a better idea. Tuwoh continued to refuse and became even more obstinate."

Yamba Farangoh took another break, sipped his cane juice that burnt his throat and yelled a few eulogies. Everyone waited eagerly for him to continue. One could have heard a pin drop. Yamba Farangoh picked up the story again.

"Kemah got so tired of her mate's foolishness that she decided to go and jump into the river and try to retrieve the fan. Everyone in Nyumodu told her that it was a stupid idea, but she insisted, and on a bright sunny day the shaker players and drummers accompanied her to the banks of Dakah.

"A huge crowd had gathered there, and Kemah left her children with her parents in case she did not return. Dancing to the rhythms of the drummers and the shaker players, she plunged into the river and completely disappeared from sight. In the water, she saw a cleared path. A voice told her to follow it and she would find a child sitting in a fan. She was to take them both home. Kemah did just that, and after retrieving the child and fan, she found herself floating on the water. The onlookers helped her onto the dry river bank with the fan and the mysterious child. The dancers, singers, and onlookers were amazed at her bravery.

"At Chief Nyuma's court once more, Kemah explained what had happened when she plunged into the deepest part of the river. Tuwoh now told the chief that since the child was found inside her fan, it was hers, as well. Not many of the villagers agreed with her, insisting that the child was Kemah's and only the fan was hers. This conflict was never resolved.

"Who should own this child?" Yamba Farangoh asked his audience. Some, like Chief Sombo, said Kemah, while others said Tuwoh, because the child was found in her fan. Who should have owned the child is still an unanswered question in that Kissi Chiefdom in Sierra Leone.

Yamba Farangoh's story was followed by huge applause from the elders and mourners. They described him as one of the most gifted griots in their midst, and he remains a legend to this day.

Chief Sombo thanked Yamba Farangoh for his clever story and the conviviality continued until the elders changed the subject and moved on to the next item on the agenda of the burial ceremony.

Chapter 7

Tewah Korfeh Is Laid to Rest

Chief Ketor asked Chief Tengbeh to tell him about the condition of the corpse, which was now lying in the courthouse, so they could start preparing it for burial. Chief Tengbeh then thanked Chief Ketor and the other elders, touched the corpse gently, and told them that it had been bathed, neatly wrapped in a newly woven country-cloth, and laid in state. It was guarded by the many priestesses in Ngaingah and by mourners from distant villages. They had bathed her, braided her hair and painted her face, because Tewah had been a priestess. All priestesses wore a piece of white cloth and were barefoot. They looked pretty, graceful, and solemn, and one could see on their faces their love for Tewah. They giggled a little when Yamba Farangoh called them the 'birds of Kissi-Kama Chiefdom.' They also had argued among themselves when Yamba Farangoh finished his story about who should have had the bouncing baby found in Tuwoh's fan, but they slowly sang the dirge of the dead, while the elders were engaged in performing the appropriate rites.

The sun now stood high in a clear blue sky. The Kissi were very mindful of the location of the sun during the day, for it was their clock. They never had any piece of paper showing how or when they should perform their ceremonies, yet they did them exactly on time and made no mistakes.

They were now approaching the most important parts of the ceremonies for the burial of Tewah. Knowing that the time had come, the priestesses started performing their sacred duties, slowly singing the dirges while dancing to the shakers, drums, and samba. They went all around the village as a group, dancing wildly. They entered the home of their most famous psychic, Fenbandu (Lasting Life), who spread a mysterious powder on their faces.

Meanwhile, Chief Ketor again stood and gathered the ample folds of his country-cloth gown and said with authoritative calmness, "Chief Tengbeh, today I have seen the well-prepared corpse that lies in my presence. With the power vested in me, I would like to request that the village give the corpse to the spirits."

"Chief Ketor has made an important request that has to be fulfilled immediately," Chief Sombo said to Chief Tengbeh and the other elders of Ngaingah.

"Yes, I will see to it at once," replied Chief Tengbeh.

"There should be a shiny object to represent the spirit of the dead," interjected Yambasu, an elder from a distant village..

"Yes, we know that. Thank you very much, Yambasu," Chief Sombo said.

The elders in Ngaingah then took a piece of iron in the form of a small spear, which was used as a medium of exchange during that colonial time, and laid it gently on the corpse. Although the dancing continued in the village, according to custom, there was silence in the courthouse until Chief Ketor broke it by saying, "Well, thank you very much, Ngaingah, for finally releasing Tewah to the spirits. It is now time to start the actual burial ceremony."

. He stood up, puffed his pipe, and nodded his head, while Yamba Farangoh yelled some eulogies, calling him 'the elephant of Kissi-Kama.'

"I have seen the present for the spirits," Chief Ketor continued. "Can we now see the husband and family of the deceased?"

"Yes, Chief Ketor," Chief Tengbeh replied politely and called Korfeh, who sat in a corner, his eyes brimming with tears.

Yamba Farangoh yelled, "Ah, Korfeh, a man can't cry his guts out. Leave crying to the women. *They* know how to cry." He silenced the crowd cunningly, and there were even some titters in the courthouse as Chief Tengbeh presented Korfeh and his children to Chief Ketor.

Chief Ketor said, "Thank you, Chief Tengbeh, Korfeh, Ngaingah, and Kissi-Kama. We have decided to bury your wife today with a ritual not seen in our chiefdom for a long time. Your wife was 'a child of the river' and also 'a child of the leaves.' That is why this burial ceremony is so unique. We have combined the rituals of both circumstances. Now, Korfeh, do you agree for your wife to be buried in Ngaingah today?"

"Eh! Massar," Korfeh replied.

"Thank you, Korfeh. You and your children should say the last words to Tewah, after which we can proceed with the final burial rites."

Crying bitterly, Korfeh gently touched his wife's corpse and said, "God has called you away at this stage in our lives, and may you be in the mighty hands of the same God. You left us still loving you. We hope that you will be loved by the spirits of our great forebears. You shall meet them ahead of you. All your children are here, and they are all wishing you a successful trip to the home of the dead. Tewah, my love is still fresh in my heart for you."

Tewah's children, grandchildren, and great-grandchildren cried and cried as they touched her face. It was a pitiful sight, and Yamba Farangoh yelled some sorrowful eulogies. In times of sorrow, these griots tried to pacify the situation with witty statements but speaking from his heart this time, Yamba Farangoh said, "Death is a road that we all shall walk on. When we come to that road, no one knows what actually takes place, Only God the almighty. No one should cry when a good woman or man dies, because while we sit here crying like babies, they are up in 'Aljeneh' (Heaven) smiling down at us."

Chief Ketor stood up again and continued the proceedings. "Chiefs and elders, the corpse is in our hands. After the priestesses have performed the final rites, we shall accompany it to the graveside." That suggestion was approved by the other elders, who sat in the court, sipping their wine, sharing some kola nuts, and chatting.

The priestesses called Fenbandu, and she stood tall in front of them. They took calabashes with mysterious contents which they sprinkled all over the village. They said this would drive out the evil spirits and maintain peace in Ngaingah. Fenbandu carried the tail of some unknown animal and shook it as she spoke to the huge crowd that had gathered. The drums and sambas throbbed, and Fenbandu danced. She laid the strange tail on the corpse and recited some incantations as if inviting the dead to speak to her.

Yamba Farangoh eulogized her to be 'a dragon among the Kissi,' for her remarkable psychic powers were well-known. The priestesses sang the songs of the dead. They danced the dance of the dead and recited incantations only the dead could understand. It was a frightening ceremony. Mothers and fathers held tightly to their children and watched it with awe. Gunfire echoed all around while the dancing continued non-stop.

The domestic animals that usually roamed freely in Ngaingah became so nervous that they stationed themselves on the outskirts of the village. Only the dogs, pigs, and cats were visible, and even they moved between the mourners with great caution. Some drunken mourners cried out to the dead from remote parts of the village, telling them to rest in peace.

Fenbandu and her priestesses had finished their part in the burial for the time being. They presented the corpse to the chiefs again by silently reciting an incantation over it to appease the dead. They then left the courthouse and returned to Fenbandu's home.

"Aha! Ngaingah, thank you so much for fulfilling these rites today. It's now time for the elders and others to pray, sing, and recite their final farewells to the dead," Chief Ketor said.

The chiefs and elders stood up and spread their arms in front of them. Chief Ketor asked Chief Sombo to bless the corpse, which he did by repeating an incantation over and over again, until he finally grew tired and returned the ceremony to Chief Ketor.

After thanking him, Chief Ketor summoned the hunters, who had continued blasting their cannons, to stand in the courthouse. Chief Ketor then opened a sack and took out a brand new country-cloth that Paramount Chief Jabba (Memah) had sent to cover the dead woman before she was put in the grave. The country-cloth was presented to Chief Sombo, who prayed on it and showed it to the other elders who touched it. Chief Sombo then opened it for all the mourners to see. The crowd cheered in acknowledgement of the kindness of their paramount chief, for the country-cloth was sacred to the Kissi and usually worn only by chiefs and other venerable elders. It was also made into a secret armor against witches, gunshots, and wild animals, especially the boa constrictors that roamed the countryside.

The sun was now moving toward the west, and the elders, mindful of the time as they looked up at the sky, adjusted the agenda of the burial ceremony accordingly. It was Kongotibo's turn to perform. She led the shaker players with a voice so rare that it seemed to penetrate the hearts of her listeners. Yamba Farangoh called her 'the toucan of Kissi-Kama.' She suddenly surged forward from the other singers and drummers, yelling eulogies for the deceased. All the mourners cheered for her.

Since the grave was now ready for the burial, Chief Ketor stood up and thanked the elders, the people of Ngaingah, and the many visiting mourners present. He then called on Chief Tengbeh to accompany the deceased to the graveside, signifying yet another phase of the burial ceremony. Hunters were called forward and, after placing the corpse on the stretcher again, respectfully took it to the graveside. There were more blasts from the cannons, and the drummers and singers again went into action. Many mourners were petrified by the continuous blasting of the gun. Babies cried in the arms of their mothers, who rocked them gently and sang sweet lullabies to put them to sleep or tied them to their backs.

Chief Sombo, Chief Ketor, and the other elders started the final burial rites. They went to the grave and prayed over it with incantations. Yamba Farangoh yelled for silence but the blasts from the cannons continued. The members of the family of the deceased were called forward, and Chief Ketor told them that it was now time to bury the dead. The drums rolled and the shakers raised their voices. The family of the deceased cried bitterly. The women wiped their faces with their head-ties, and the counselors consoled them by reminding them gently that no one fights against destiny. The mourners stood sadly by, some crying too. Korfeh agreed for the corpse of his late wife to be buried.

Sakillah, the lead hunter who had overseen the digging of the grave, stood up and told the elders that it was ready for the burial. The corpse was respectfully handed over to Chief Sombo by Chief Tengbeh. Chief Sombo then passed it respectfully to Chief Ketor. The drums and shakers played continuously. Yamba Farangoh responded with a few eulogies.

Chief Ketor said, "To all elders and mourners in Ngaingah, I stand before you today as your humble servant and to represent our most respected Paramount Chief Memah. I have been given the opportunity by Chief Sombo, his council of elders, along with Korfeh and his entire family to bury Tewah Korfeh. Everyone knows Tewah Korfeh was 'a child of the river' and at the same time 'a child of the leaves.' We have treasured all the love shown for the last two days. We have cried, danced, eaten, and drunk our Tamba Nanjah. Now we are about to bury the dead."

Yamba Farangoh yelled and remarked that the drunken men and women sprawled in the corners of the village were a clear indication of the might of the Tamba Nanjah. This made the mourners giggle despite their sorrow.

Chief Ketor continued, "Tewah Korfeh's soul rests in peace."

"Amee-nah!" the huge large crowd answered.

The elders gathered again. They hung their heads together in secret conversation. The 'choire-epae-yah' leaves were brought, and they prayed over them once more.

"Tewah's absence in Ngaingah has created a vacuum in their lives." Chief Sombo said. Kongotibo and her shaker players eulogized the late Tewah Korfeh and sang the songs she loved to dance to in her lifetime.

Gifts and other belongings of the deceased were brought in boxes. Finda, Tewah's daughter, was selected to be the next Tewah Korfeh in Ngaingah by the priestesses. This had significant meaning in their culture. Finda was now going to assume all the responsibilities of her late mother in Ngaingah and in Kissi-Kama.

The priestesses had reassembled on the outskirts of Ngaingah and slowly sang the songs of the dead. They had painted their faces again and looked frightening as they stood in a line. The dogs barked. The cocks crowed, and toucans on distant palm trees hooted intermittently. All these signified that the spirit of dead was welcome in the home of the dead. The drummers and shakers played mysterious rhythms and the singers sang the same songs sung by the priestesses. Everyone fell silent. The sound of the cannons continued to echo around the hill, and the mourners looked on with uneasy countenances. It was again a frightening scene which scared the children.

The priestesses came and surrounded the corpse. They knelt beside it and prayed by reciting some incantations that only the dead could understand. They sang and sang. The elders simply waited. The drummers played. The priestesses then stood slowly and, in single file, headed for the forest and did not return to Ngaingah until after the burial, because they were not to see 'a child of the river,' and 'a child of the leaves' buried. That was the law.

Kongotibo sang a song that introduced a little humor even around the graveside. All the mourners knew it and joined in, singing the words slowly.

The elders expressed concern over what was to be put in the grave and after a rapid discussion, Chief Ketor sent two men to put into it all the items that should accompany the corpse, according to custom. Among these items were gunpowder and some sacred objects that only the elders and priestesses could justify.

By now, the crying had reached its peak. Several times the children of the deceased fell on the dusty ground and kicked up their feet crying bitterly. The counselors again consoled them, but they couldn't be consoled. Chief Ketor recited an incantation over a bottle of gin and poured its contents beside the grave to appease the spirits of dead. He then invited everyone who wanted to say something before the corpse was finally put in the grave to do so. Many with teary eyes came forward, but they just stood there crying and had to be held back. Kongotibo now sang and played the shakers with vigor. Her backers echoed tunefully.

After the proper traditional procedure, Chief Ketor signaled for the corpse to be placed in the grave. The two men, who had previously gone in, now climbed out as gunshots continued to echo around them. The elders poured the 'choire-epae-yah' leaves into the grave and after that signaled to the hunters to pour in the earth. All the mourners knew that it was the final ritual when the elders again recited some incantations and poured gin on the grave as a libation. Chief Sombo then thanked Chief Ketor profusely for the culturally perfect funeral they had conducted with his guidance.

Ketor was hailed as Paramount Chief Memah's greatest emissary. After dancing, drinking, and sleeping that night in Ngaingah, he and his entourage left for Dia the next day. The grateful people of Ngaingah sent the paramount chief some live domestic animals, tins of palm oil, bags of cleaned rice, and many other items not disclosed to the public. The village also provided porters to take the goods to Dia, the headquarters of Kissi-Kama Chiefdom.

Chief Sombo and his elders accompanied Chief Ketor only as far as a small tributary of the Ndopie, for in Kissi culture it was forbidden for members of a bereaved family to cross a river when seeing off visiting mourners. For the same reason, they did not look back after saying goodbye but went on to the Ndopie shrine to lay kola nuts and pour some libations.

On their way back to Ngaingah, they talked about the funeral, concluding that it had been one of the most successful in the Kissi-Kama Chiefdom. Ahead of them on the dusty footpath, Chief Sombo spotted a small green mamba. Such snakes were common in shrines and in rivers but not usually on footpaths. It lay curled on the footpath, undisturbed by their presence, even when they stood beside it. That made them realize that it was the late Tewah Korfeh's spirit that had appeared to them. She was trying to show to them that she had appreciated what Ngaingah did for her. Chief Sombo recited an incantation, and the snake disappeared. This is another example of how involved in magic the Kissi were. It was so amazing that the other chiefs praised Chief Sombo who was indeed a mystic in his day.

After the ceremonies, a stream of mourners continued to leave Ngaingah to return to their villages. It was several weeks before life returned to normal and Chief Sombo could once again lie in his hammock, take catnaps, tell the children stories, puff at his pipe, and blow smoke into the ceiling of his courthouse.

Chapter 8

Farming in Ngaingah

The dry season in Ngaingah was now at its peak. The bush was so dry that a flash of thunder could have ignited a fire which was exactly what the Kissi wanted. In the farming season, the bush was deliberately set on fire to burn large acres of farmland that they would later cultivate with rice, cassava, yams, and all sorts of vegetables. The burning of the bushes during the farming season was done with a lot of humor and enthusiasm.

Areas of the villages where coffee and cacao plantations and banana trees grew were well protected from these fierce bush fires by controlling the blaze, and the villagers never allowed the fires to consume the areas of human habitation. But the fires had benefits too. When they had died down, the hunters and villagers followed their paths, searching for animal carcasses left behind. The hunters watched with their guns at-a-ready for any animals that might have escaped the blaze and hidden in the undergrowth.

After the death of Tewah Korfeh, the farmers in Ngaingah had successfully burned large acres of farmland. They then waited for the first rains to fall and soften the soil, so they could begin plowing with hoes made by the local blacksmiths.

Gbekah was one of the most renowned blacksmiths in Kissi-Kama. In his workshop in Ngaingah, he manufactured gunpowder as well as hoes, knives, and machetes which he supplied to the farmers in the chiefdom. To make these utensils, he heated iron bars on glowing coals produced with his huge bellows, and then hit them with all his strength, using a big hammer. Gbekah and his son, Sahr, were now the busiest blacksmiths in Ngaingah, since all the local farmers and those from most of the surrounding villages ordered new hoes from his workshop or brought their old ones to be sharpened.

Farming brought the villagers together, and they laid their farms in close proximity. The farmers would meet, chat, drink, and work together. The Kissi usually used a group-plowing method by assisting individual households one at a time. Plowing was done by the men while the women walked behind them with forked-sticks, which they used to scratch the ground, loosening the dirt, and removing unwanted grass left behind by the plowmen. After the rains fell, the work could be done more easily because the soil was so soft.

On Chief Sombo's farm, the work was going on at a frantic pace. The last rains had fallen a few days before, so the soil was now very soft. Chief Sombo invited Kongotibo, his beloved shaker player, and her backers, whom he called her 'singings birds,' to his farm. Their melodious songs echoing around early on a bright sunny day had signaled that plowing was beginning in Ngaingah. Each plowman's name was called out. Some of them echoed the "Ho! Ho! Ho!" of the white man's Santa Claus when their names were eulogized by 'the singing birds,' and they began to pulverize the loose soil with the strength of Samson. These men went from farm to farm and could plow almost any size of farm in one day.

Chief Sombo took a few elders and sat under a large, shady tree. He poured Tambah Nangah gin on the bare ground and recited an incantation to thank God and the ancestors for a bountiful harvest to come, for protection, and for answering their prayers all the year round.

A headman walked in front of the plowmen. He took a bit of husk rice and scattered it ahead of the plowmen who then tilled the soft soil. The work was laborious, but the Kissi did it with energy, song, dance, and humor. Even snakebites didn't discourage them from doing their work which they carried on until the sun stood high in the sky. Only then did the farmers retire to get some rest and eat. The plowmen ate from large wooden bowls, while Kongotibo and her group of singers entertained them with songs and the shakers. Then they too retired for awhile. The laborious work ended at dusk, and Chief Sombo again entertained them in the village with food and drink.

When the rice seedlings germinated, the work of the women began. They spent more time on the farm than the men, removing by hand the weeds that germinated with the seedlings and then nursing the plants until they were ready for harvesting. The women worked with sweet songs and lullabies.

Tengbeh was one of the hard-working men during Chief Sombo's days in Ngaingah. His son, Kendema, had been bitten by a viper on the farm, and Chief Sombo, who happened to be near the farm at the time, was summoned urgently. He immediately went to work, pricking the wound and applying a mysterious black substance. The small crowd that had gathered watched the entire episode in awed silence. Kendema's pain disappeared immediately, and it wasn't long before he stood on his feet and returned to work. He even climbed palm trees and harvested a few kegs of wine which he presented to Chief Sombo on that day.

During the farming season in Ngaingah, the village remained deserted during the day. Only the old remained there. Even infants were taken along and camped out in the barns. The mothers breastfed them and then left them in the care of their little sisters and brothers while they went back to work.

After work on the dry soil was completed, the farmers then planted rice nurseries in the swamps to be harvested later. They took the rice seedlings and neatly submerged them on the spongy mats of decayed plants or on swampy surfaces. Although they sometimes used hoes to plant seedlings, they used cutlasses or machetes to brush the swamp. The planting of the rice nurseries in the swamp was done barefoot, so blood-sucking insects enjoyed the flesh of these farmers as they worked. The swampy ground also hid poisonous reptiles.

As soon as the rice seedlings burst from their stems, the men went to work, erecting snares all around the farms to catch the destructive nocturnal animals that came to eat the succulent rice seedlings. The inventive Kissi made all types of snares and for all types of animals, even boa constrictors. To tackle the palm birds who came to eat the rice seedlings, the farmers also manufactured slings by peeling palm fronds, weaving the threads into long ropes, and tying a pocket-like pouch to the ends of the long ropes. They could throw stones considerable distances with these slings, thus scaring the birds away. They invented another method of scaring birds which was to hang long ropes all over the farms. When shaken, the ropes scared the birds away. During the bird-scaring season, from dawn to dusk, the men and boys spent much of their time on high stands, scaring the birds away.

During the planting season, a man called Focko clashed with Wango, one of his younger wives. Their bitter quarrel continued all night. Wango had screamed so loudly from the punches she received from Focko's mighty fists that their neighbors intervened. That was how tumultuous a polygamous relationship could sometimes be.

At dawn, Chief Sombo summoned the couple to his courthouse and asked Focko to explain what had happened, since in the Kissi tradition it was a sign of respect that a chief ask the husband to speak before the wife.

"Why did you wake Ngaingah up so early, Focko?" Chief Sombo inquired.

"Well, Chief Sombo, my younger wife, Wango, has been uncooperative at home lately. She decided to disrespect her mates, who are her seniors, and to be a hot-head at home," Focko answered.

"He is lying, Massar Sombo. He is not telling the truth in your court," Wango told the chief with tears in her eyes.

"Wango, don't tell your husband that he is lying in my court," Chief Sombo rebuked her.

"I am sorry, Massar Sombo," Wango said.

"Your apology is accepted. Now allow your husband to air his grievances against you. After which, you will have your chance," Chief Sombo told her.

"My apologies, Massar Sombo," Wango reiterated.

"Accepted, Wango," Chief Sombo again responded.

Focko sighed and said with disdain, "She doesn't mean it, Chief Sombo."

To calm the situation, the chief then told them to respect his authority. Wango looked away, rolling her eyes at her husband in a most disrespectful way.

Focko removed his snuffbox from one of the many pockets in his huge country-cloth gown, pinched some tobacco, and hid it inside his mouth.

Chief Sombo continued smoking his pipe, enjoying the drama unfolding in his court. He took out a piece of white kola nut, broke it, and split it between Focko and Wango as a sign that he wanted a peaceful resolution to the family argument.

Wango then bowed her head and began to shed copious tears. Tengbeh, who had just entered the court, consoled her.

"Stop crying, Wango," he said. "Tell us what really happened between you and your husband."

Wango swallowed her sobs and wiped her face. She knew that her husband loved her exceedingly and that the altercation was caused by jealousy.

"Massar Sombo and all the elders here today, my husband Focko is a very jealous man. He has accused me many times of having an affair with Tengbeh's son, Kendema," Wango replied, starting to sob again. "I have denied the allegation over and over, but he has persisted in the accusation until we have found ourselves in this ugly situation today."

Chief Sombo and his council of elders now saw the case from a different angle. It smelt of lies, jealousy, and punishment, and they realized that they needed some time to investigate it thoroughly. Since the sun was now high in the sky, Wango was told to stay with Tuwoh, until the farmers returned home in the evening when the case would be settled.

It later transpired that the quarrel began when Kendema's and his friend, Fayia, went to play 'see-yon-yee-yoh' or the 'tie-the-seeds' under a kola nut tree. It is a game played by men sitting face to face. The men 'tie-the-seeds' on a dented mound and the seed remaining at the end, wins. Afterwards they decided to climb the tree to pick some nuts. It was there that Fayia mentioned to Focko that Wango had told a friend that she had fallen in love with Kendema. On hearing this, Focko went and attacked Wango, demanding that she confess. She denied the allegation and the fighting began.

The Kissi encourage long-lasting marriages, which was why they gave so much as dowry—money in the form of a small iron spear, goods, and even domestic animals. No one could repay such large dowries. If the wife confessed to unfaithfulness, she lay prostrate on the ground, and her husband touched her as a sign of forgiveness. But, before that took place, some husbands beat their wives so mercilessly that the chief or the elders had to intervene.

Wango's case was quite different though, because she had not actually been unfaithful to Focko. She told the truth to Tuwoh who relayed the confession to her husband. As expected, Wango lay prostrate on the ground and apologized. The chief then counseled Wango and Focko and promised to tell Kendema to leave them alone.

When Chief Sombo later returned to his court, he told Tengbeh about Wango's confession regarding his son, Kendema. Tengbeh then summoned his son who came and curtsied before the elders. He was then told to sit next to Chief Sombo and did so, listening attentively with anxious ears and expressive eyes.

Chief Sombo was known for speaking his mind and fearing no one, but he saw anxiety in Kendema's eyes and gently informed him he had been summoned to discourage him from having an affair with Wango, Focko's wife, who had confessed his name on the same day. Kendema looked perplexed and shook his head in denial. His countenance showed great concern. "Kekeh (Father) Sombo, this woman has accused me falsely," Kendema said.

"Well, Kendema, I wasn't there, so do I know what exactly took place? Anyway, since she confessed your name, and you are our son, it's better that you leave her alone and desist from such funny business, especially with married women in Ngaingah," Chief Sombo admonished him sternly.

"Thank you, Kekeh Sombo," Kendema said humbly.

Not long after that, Chief Sombo paid an unannounced visit to Tengbeh's farm, because the time had come to harvest the palm and bamboo wines; also the rice harvesting season was now approaching. He and Tengbeh sat on a heavy log that lay on the farm, having informed the sling throwers where they were, for it was dangerous to roam about the farms when stones were flying in all directions. Accidents were rare though, because the Kissi took great care during the bird-scaring season.

They drank wine and poured a few drops on the ground to appease the spirits of their forebears who had helped them reap an abundance of rice. As they drank and talked, they heard the chirps and whistles of the birds and watched the sun descending to the western horizon. Its rays were delightfully gentle at that time of day. When dusk signaled, everyone returned to the village.

Chapter 9

Harvesting the New Rice

The Kissi knew that the rice had reached the point of harvesting when the color of the stalks changed from green to yellow. Here, too, the blacksmiths were important, for they manufactured the small knives that were used to reap the rice by slicing it from the long stems. Farmers in distant villages such as Kondoma, Njah, Yeibeima, Lewoing, Sarkpeh, and Mano Sewadu had already started harvesting, since they had laid their farms earlier.

It wasn't long before the farmers in Ngaingah started harvesting the rice on their own farms. They had already sent messages to the reapers-for-hire in the Kissi-Kama Chiefdom to come to their aid. Reapers-for-hire were ordinary villagers who lived in the chiefdom and came together during the harvesting season to do this work. Poor farmers who were not in a position to hire them did their own harvesting.

Temperatures became unbearable at this time of the year, but the Kissi never allowed that to bother them and did their job with humor. At harvest time, the young women harvested some sheaves of rice that they quickly dried in large fans. They then heated the husk rice on hot pots by stirring it with long wooden spoons before pounding it in mortars to produce rice flour. This was the rice flour that was given to their lovers with few kola nuts to signify their love. One could hear these young men boasting that their girlfriends have made them rice flour with the newly harvested rice. During the harvesting season, lovers renewed their vows. This took place in the moonlight on the farm and in the village. It was also in the moonlight that the children of Ngaingah played the 'duduleng' or hide-and-seek, in which a boy was chosen to look for his friends who had hidden behind the many domestic animals and in the remote corners of the village. Anyone the boy touched had to take his place.

The young girls came together to play and dance by clapping their hands. They stepped with their feet in intricate patterns to match the clapping. They also sang songs and danced to them. Most of these young girls later became great singers. Some of the young women sat beside the old near the fires and listened to their stories, most of which followed sweet songs.

Ngaingah on a moonlit night was a joyful place to be but on one a moonlit night, the children spotted a huge rock python lying quietly on the main footpath that led to the village from Dia. It was very strange for a reptile to come so near villages, since the Kissi had magic potions to stop them from doing so. The boys ran to Chief Sombo's court and reported what they had seen. The chief then summoned Tungofullah and the other hunters to hunt it down and, knowing that it was a sacred reptile, gave permission for them to kill it.

Nyuma was the trusted hunter in this instance, for he was known to have killed many rock pythons. He had massive hands; everyone in Ngaingah knew that he was the strongest man in the village.

Chief Sombo summoned him and as soon as he had talked to the chief, he hurried home, took his gun and knife, and put on his sacred country-cloth which made him invincible in times of danger. That sacred shirt had magical powers. Nyuma could kill a lion, an elephant, or a tiger when he wore that shirt. He walked like a giant to the chief's court, followed by the other hunters. All of them went hurriedly to where the rock python had already swallowed a goat and lay curled under a kola nut tree.

The reptile was so full that it could hardly move an inch, even when the audacious hunters closed in on it. Nyuma touched his gun, knowing that he had enough gunpowder to kill the snake.

The reptile looked balefully at the hunters. Nyuma decided to split its massive stomach with his knife as it lay helpless and at the mercy of the most fearless men in Kissi-Kama.

A crowd of villagers stood at a distance and watched the scene as it unfolded under brilliant moonlight. Nyuma ordered his colleagues to hold the huge tail of the reptile, and the deadly struggle began. The reptile was no match for the hunters. They recited an incantation which made the bulky creature lie so limply that even an infant could have killed it. The scary scene sent shivers down the spines of the villagers who stood and watched as Nyuma plunged his long knife into the massive belly of the reptile. It burst open and the goat it had earlier swallowed fell to the ground.

It was a tradition that when such sacred animals and reptiles were killed, the chiefs and elders blessed it with special incantations before the meat was consumed, so Chief Sombo and the elders were called. Though some Kissi considered eating python meat a taboo, others enjoyed it, saying its soft flesh resembled that of a fish. Part of the meat was also sent to Paramount Chief Jabba at Dia.

Having reached the peak of its brilliance, the moon was fading as the villagers entered their huts to rest before the hectic day on the farms that lay ahead of them. Some of the children had fearful dreams about the snake, so after that incident they were told to play near the huts and not to go to the outskirts of the village.

Harvesting had already commenced on farms in Ngaingah, and Chief Sombo had selected a day for the hired reapers to work on his farm. He had already invited the griot, Yambo Farangoh, to add color and life to the proceedings. The most renowned comedian and praise singer of the time, Yamba Farangoh, improvised comic sketches to suit the occasion. It made his listeners laugh so much that their stomachs ached.

Chief Sombo also summoned Kongotibo, the most talented singer and shaker player, from Sondokollohbendu village. However, she couldn't come to his farm because she had already been invited by another paramount chief to perform on his farms. These great drummers and singers sometimes composed their songs on the spot. Since Kongotibo wasn't available, Chief Sombo invited Komeh and his drummers from Buedu in the Kissi-Tongui Chiefdom. The night they arrived, the moon shone brilliantly, and the chief invited everyone to his courthouse to be entertained, to chat, and to prepare for the harvest. After they had been shown their accommodations, the singers and drummers performed with unbridled enthusiasm. Some domestic animals had been killed, and the women were already engaged in steaming the meat to make it tender so that the next day's cooking could be done easily.

Early the next morning, the harvesters, singers, and a huge crowd converged on Chief Sombo's farm. The reapers had left first. They attacked the harvesting after reciting some incantations. No one could decipher the meaning of these mysterious words but after the ceremony, the reapers did their work like machines. Even to this day, the Kissi ask themselves how these men got the strength to harvest sheaves of rice like machines.

Komeh and his drummers raised their voices in song. They eulogized Chief Sombo, who was carrying a long sword with which he cleared the bush, and performed a magical dance. They called him the 'lion of Kissi-Kama,' also an 'elephant and a boa constrictor.'

Yamba Farangoh sat at a vantage point on a big rock where he was seen by all the farmers. He had earlier spied a viper, but he just smiled at it and called out to Chief Sombo, who came and caught it with his bare hands, and then put it in the sack he always carried. Yamba Farangoh then enlivened the proceedings with a few sharp eulogies, calling out the names of the ordinary reapers and giving them flattering aliases. Each reaper that he called fired back with a 'Ho! Ho! Ho!' to show that he was present and thanked Yamba Farangoh for recognizing him.

As soon as Yamba Farangoh yelled, the crowd went wild. Laughter and noisy applause echoed as far as the distant horizons. He also told funny stories which sometimes ended with humorous songs that only a gifted interpreter of proverbs could decipher. The hired reapers remained mute, working like machines throughout. It was impossible for the human eye to follow the accuracy and speed with which their hands performed their job. The cowry shells on their long hats shook according to the rhythm of the songs sung by the women behind them, but they neither spoke nor stopped to drink water until they rested. Their work began with the rising of the sun and ended when the sun set. People said that it never rained when they worked on any farm, because they had special charms and amulets which they concealed in the short country-cloth gowns they wore.

The harvest in Ngaingah was accomplished with such a compelling display of cultural practices, local talent, and group cooperation that it attracted farmers from all around. They loved the lively and inspiring atmosphere on the farm and came to praise Chief Sombo for being such a great organizer. Some came from distant villages to see the wonderful reapers and share in the fun, bringing with them gifts such as kola nuts, oranges, mangoes, guavas, and bananas to add to the food already available in sufficient quantities. Palm wine and gin flowed in abundance.

Chief Sombo and the other farmers walked behind the reapers, but all they had to do was to tie the sheaves of rice into small bundles which they gave to the women to take to the village and stack in barns.

That year Ngaingah was blessed with so much rice that the barns overflowed with it. Individual families went to the shrines and oracles to pour libation to the spirits of their forebears and thank the Almighty God for such a bountiful harvest. No one recited more incantations than Chief Sombo. He could go on for five minutes, and all the listeners had to say was, "Amee-nah!" over and over again.

The harvesting season also gave rise to some extremely hard work for the women. They had to take the sheaves of rice and dry them in long fans in the sun. When the husk rice dropped from the dried stems, they put it in mortars and pounded it till it was clean. This was a daily task and the only way to feed their families. The pounding sometimes made them dizzy. One can imagine the problem for a woman who might be suffering from high blood pressure. The swamp rice was harvested after the upland rice and didn't lead to much celebration even though its cultivation had its own problems. Not only were the farmers menaced by blood-sucking worms but also by the noisy, stinging insects that circled above their heads and sat on their bare bodies. Yet, they went about their business as if nothing was happening. They were encouraged by the swarms of butterflies that rested gently on their heads and on other parts of their bodies as if to appease them for the discomfort, which included toads and frogs, drumming in their ears with unending choruses, while toucans (belanbelando) hooted "Baa! Baa! Baa!" in the distant palm trees.

Chapter 10

Fishing in the Ndopie River

After the harvesting season, the women of Ngaingah went on fishing expeditions. They were skillful in making large vertical nets, called seines, which they hung over their shoulders on fishing expeditions while the men went hunting. Small baskets neatly woven from raffia palms were tied on the women's heads.

Tuwoh Sombo organized the women's fishing expeditions in Ngaingah. All the women who participated in such expeditions listened to her instructions. Like her husband, Chief Sombo, she was an organizer of repute but charming and kind. She taught the women how to weave seines from palm leaves with intricate patterns in the form of a spider's web. The palm leaves were removed from their stalks and peeled to produce ropes which were then used to weave the nets. It sometimes took a month to make a neat fishing net, but the women persevered and succeeded in manufacturing many of them. A long rattan was used to form the circle which held the finished net in place.

Tuwoh Sombo went from hut to hut to inform the women of Ngaingah about the day they were to go on a fishing expedition, then with Tuwoh presiding, they met in Chief Sombo's courthouse the evening before to launch their expedition. They remarked that the next day was expected to be cool, sunny, and calm, though they sometimes went fishing during the rainy season.

The next morning as the sun rose gently in the clear sky, Tuwoh could be heard calling out their names, "Yawah, Finda, Sia, Tewa, Kumba, Wango, Dambi and

Koloh." Anyone she called answered, "e-cho-nang." (I'm present). With the group now assembled, Tuwoh led them on the footpath and through the cacao and coffee plantations on the outskirts of Ngaingah to the site where the fishing was to take place. By then the sun would be high enough to shine brilliantly through the foliage of the cacao and coffee trees.

During their fishing expeditions, Tuwoh and her friends enjoyed the many chirping birds and the company and mischief of the monkeys. If they spotted a tiny green snake, they knew that it was a good sign and were not afraid. On that fishing expedition, Tuwoh also remembered the late Tewah Korfeh who used to be active on such occasions. She and Tewah had grown up together in Ngaingah. As little girls, they were among those who went to beg the gods to bless them with big breasts under the "Lamboo-Lamboo" tree. The girls and young women went to dance under the tree, begging it to give them big breasts as they sang this song:

> "Lamboo-Lamboo give me your big breasts
> And take my small breasts.'
> "Lamboo-Lamboo give me your big breasts
> And take the my small breasts"
> (Repeat)

As the women made their way down to the river, they were pricked painfully by hundreds of thorns when they passed by unbrushed shrubs on their way down the slippery and muddy bank. Tuwoh pointed to the spot where they were going to start fishing, as if she knew exactly where they would find fish. Then they stood in a semicircle in the muddy river and pushed their seines from one bank to the other. Just before they touched the edge of the other bank, they raised the nets to collect crabs, fish, shrimps, and whatever else they found in them. Sometimes they caught large river snakes but not boa constrictors. The fish and crabs fought bravely to be returned to the river, but the women took them and put them inside the small baskets tied on the side of their heads. Tuwoh then pointed to another location. While they fished, they were attacked by blood-sucking insects that landed on their flesh.

They sang uplifting traditional songs while they fished. The men could hear them singing in Ngaingah and praised them for their courage and for their excellent organization of such fishing trips. These men and the little ones had stayed home to take care of the babies and stop them crying. On the muddy ground near the huts, the boys played 'Tee-tah-too' by throwing a coin or pebble into marked circles or squares then hopping inside to gain the area hit. If the coin or pebble went astray, the next player took over.

The fishing had gone well, and the sun was now falling to the horizon. The women had made some successful catches, but they continued to make merry in the Ndopie River until dusk fell. Then, having cleaned themselves in the river and removed the debris from their skin, they returned to the village in a procession now singing ceremoniously.

Their children welcomed them, although the infants cried when they laid eyes on their mothers again. The mothers stretched out their hands to embrace and breastfeed them, while the girls cleaned the fish. The catch was then hung over the hearths to preserve it and was consumed over a couple of days.

Nyuma Sombo, one of Chief Sombo's sons encouraged his friends to go on fishing expeditions at the

Ndopie River. They never used seining but improvised fishing rods with long sticks and ropes, which they made from weaving palm leaves, and then tied a hook at the end. They searched in the muddy banks of the river or in swamps for worms which they used as bait. The boys stood there for many hours at a time until they had caught enough fish. They would then climb the kola nut trees and pick fresh nuts, which they took home for the elders who were always in the courthouse chatting and smoking their pipes, as they discussed ways to develop the village and what sacrifices needed to be made for the seasons and various occasions to come.

Chapter 11

Initiation Season

It was now initiation season in Ngaingah, for after the harvest season they were assured of a constant supply of food at the bush schools. They organized the bush school or the Sandi Society camp for girls and the Poro Society camp for boys. If the Sandi Society camp was held in Ngaingah, girls were brought in from other villages to attend. Such occasions were crowned with festivities. After graduation, the society bush was abandoned for that year. They had to wait until the following year to decide where the next society camps were going to be held, and the village that was chosen started making preparations for the initiates from enrollment to graduation.

In Ngaingah, the decision to enroll the boys, the girls, and sometimes older men was left to the relatives or individual households. Chief Sombo would earlier have informed the village about the coming enrollment. The Poro Society was encamped on the outskirts of Ngaingah, whereas the Sandi Society built the camp to lodge their initiates at the edge of the village. That site was considered extremely sacred and, as a rule, only women were allowed to go there, just as only men were allowed to go to the boys' camp. Yet, there are exceptions to every rule. The Kissi have the 'sokoah' who are considered philosophers and guides with regard to traditional customs. These men and women could enter either camp.

Some of the boys and girls to be initiated were so young that the decision to enter the camp was made by their parents and relatives. The boys cried for their mothers and the girls for their fathers because they would not see them until graduation day. What they were taught at the sacred sites has remained secret to this day, because no one was allowed to expose the secrets. In the old days, disrespecting this law carried punishments such as fines or banishment from the chiefdom. Those banished went to neighboring Guinea or to Liberia and returned only when the 'sokoah' gave them permission. Sometimes they were afraid to return to the chiefdom.

Sending initiates from neighboring villages to Ngaingah was not unusual, for the inhabitants of those distant villages knew that Chief Sombo was the best organizer of such occasions. In Kissi-Kama Chiefdom, Ngaingah was also renowned for organizing the best cultural shows and exhibitions associated with initiations. Spectators came from distant villages, bringing gifts for the initiates. Because it was the dry season, these exhibitions were held out in the open. It was also the time when the footpaths were at their most dusty since the rains had now ceased.

After calling an impromptu meeting of all the men and women who headed these societies as well as the 'sohoah,' Chief Sombo sent his village crier, Tambel-loh, to inform the villagers about plans for the initiations. Around this time, the innocent boys and girls were told all kinds of scary stories about the genie they would meet at the camps. Some of these stories even claimed that the genie was going to consume them and vomit them on the graduation day. The children became so apprehensive that some of them cried and had to be consoled by their parents who told them that all the stories were a pack of lies, but that what they witnessed at the camp was never to be revealed to anyone, not even to their mothers and fathers.

At the girls' camp, genital mutilation was done to initiate them into womanhood, but this secret would only be known to them when they entered the camp. Although westerners tried to abolish a traditional practice which had lasted over a thousand years, how genital mutilation was done remained a deep secret until recent times.

For the boys, the Poro initiation was done by scarification. These marks were inserted in the middle of their backs and up to their shoulders. They were also marked in secret places as a way of protecting them against snakes, scorpions, witches, and other evils. The initiates demonstrated great courage as weeks passed by. They were also taught how to be successful fathers and mothers and how to lay farms, harvest palm nuts, and lay snares in the forest.

Celebrations were held from the day the camps were opened until graduation. The shaker players, singers, drummers, praise singers, and griots always graced such occasions. Every night, dances were held in Ngaingah. Initiates could hear the beating of the distant drums and the songs that were sung. Knowing that they were closer to their parents encouraged them, and they behaved like young adults as they were initiated to adulthood. They were always under the watchful eyes of their educators and especially the 'sokoah,' so no one ever ran away from these camps.

Initiation was an ongoing process, since the educators never waited for anyone. The initiates who came late were taught the lessons already learnt by those who had been present earlier. At night in both the boys and the girls' initiation camp, singing lessons were held. They sang beautiful songs so loudly that their parents heard them in the village. Distant camps in distant villages replied with their own songs, and a competition ensued until the wee hours of the morning. The camp that became silent was the loser since they obviously had no more songs to sing. The griots went to the camps to teach these boys and girls the songs and history of their culture. They also taught them about medicinal herbs and the philosophy behind their traditional way of life.

Chief Sombo had made all necessary arrangements, so things were under control. He and his elders supervised the societies from the courthouse in Ngaingah. They enrolled the latecomers and sent them immediately to the camps. Graduation fees were paid in goods such as tins of palm oil, domestic animals, sacks of cleaned rice, and whatever Chief Sombo and his elders decided should be paid. They never asked for exorbitant fees, since most families couldn't afford them. That year, even Sakillah, the chief of Lepeining village, brought his son to be initiated in Ngaingah. He met Chief Sombo in the courthouse that morning and after meeting all the prerequisites for enrollment, his son was accepted and then mysteriously vanished from the courthouse only to reappear in the Poro initiation camp accompanied by a 'sokonoh' (singular of 'sokoah'). Sahr Sakillah, as he was later called, became the most gifted singer at the Poro initiation camp. His creative ability in composing songs on the spur of the moment made the Poro initiation camp in Ngaingah win all the nightly singing competitions. Sahr Sakillah became a renowned griot in Kissi-Kama in his old age.

Capturing the boys and the girls and putting them 'inside the big belly of the genie,' as the Kissi put it, continued. 'Dancing-men' and 'dancing-women' were responsible for such enrollments. Each night, the atmosphere was eerie and tense as these dancers stood at the doorsteps of the homes of the boys and girls whose families had agreed to give them up. As soon as the children emerged, a crowd of dancers encircled them, and they disappeared only to reappear in the camp.

Cooking for both societies was done in Ngaingah. At night, the genie secretly brought bundles of dry wood, from the boys' Poro camp. It was the wood used to cook the food for the initiates. The food was also mysteriously taken to the camps. It was forbidden for parents to send cooked food to the camps for their children. The women of Ngaingah continued to go on fishing expeditions during the initiation season, but with great caution so as not to be seen by the boys who had just been initiated. It was also forbidden for the women to see them.

If there were any deaths in the camp, such bad news was kept from the parents, and they were only told of such incidents on the day of the graduation. That was the reason many parents cried when their children departed and even regretted sending them to the camp. The fathers who had been initiated into the Poro Society accompanied their sons to the boys' initiation camp; the mothers who had been initiated into the Sandi Society accompanied their daughters to the girls' camp. Although most parents continued to wonder about the well-being of their children whom they couldn't see, the nights in Ngaingah continued to be cozy and enchanting. The rejoicing, fun, and mischief continued non-stop.

A few weeks after the initiations started and things were going well, the boys and girls began learning more songs and dances in the camps. Famous dancers and singers were invited from all over the chiefdom to teach them techniques of dancing for the exhibition day which also marked their graduation. They rehearsed over and over again. As the girls were now considered healthy enough to dance, their rehearsals and exhibitions were held in public in Chief Sombo's courtyard. The families, friends, and distant relatives came to watch and bring gifts. These girls, now young women, danced to the shakers, while the drummers backed them up with exquisite techniques; but when their loved ones came to see them dance, they were not allowed to look them in the eye, for they remained the property of the genie until graduation day. They could only nod to them. Seeing their daughters again excited the anxious fathers and relieved them of any emotional pain. The boys had their rehearsals too. The initiates, both boys and girls, wore skimpy raffia skirts to show that they were now in the dancing mood.

It was the time of an old man called Jimmy, who played the samba, and when Queseo (a singer) Sia Ngeleh Foryoh and her group of shaker players and singers performed during the graduation ceremonies that were held in the Kissi-Kama Chiefdom. On graduation day, all these renowned female shaker players: Sia Ngeleh Foryoh of Koindu, Kongotibo of Sondokorlloh village, Wango of Yegbadu, Kueyoh of Mendekorma, Kon-ngee of Kpandoning, and many more came together. They formed one of the most exciting groups of shaker players and singers of their time. Special stands were built for them with sticks, and there they sat and sang the melodious songs of the time. They were skillful shaker players and prolific composers. They were also gifted with proverbs and could play and sing for days at a time. Their voices seemed to grow stronger and stronger. Chief Sombo loved them. So did Paramount Chief Memah who danced to their songs.

On the day of the great graduation exhibition, the girls were dressed in strange outfits, and their faces were painted. They also wore beads of different colors around their necks and around their waists. Kpanah Cholan, the little sister of Queseo Sia Ngeleh Foryoh, was among the 'sokoah' at the girls' initiation camp. She was also an important figure in the Sandi Society. On the day of the spectacular exhibition, many families went to choose wives from among the virgins who had just been initiated. These young women were later accompanied to the homes of their husbands-to-be after the payment of a dowry.

Chiefs were presented with young concubines as gifts, and they became one of their many wives. If the girl was too young, she stayed in the family until she grew to the age when she could lose her virginity and become a wife. These intermarriages brought peace among the Kissi, and that has been the practice to this day.

On the graduation day in Ngaingah, the weather was balmy and cool. It was now the driest portion of the dry season, and dusty winds powdered the faces of the people of Ngaingah. There were many spectators. Some came to see their sisters, others their children, while many just came to see the painted faces of the beautiful girls who now had protruding breasts and shapely buttocks that the young men loved.

Chief Sombo had gone to consult the famous Fenbandu who was now the most trusted psychic in Ngaingah. She also headed the sect of mysteriously gifted women who were priestesses. The chief had gone to ask her to use her psychic powers to see if the graduation day was going to be a success in Ngaingah.

Fenbandu solemnly sat on a mat woven from dried raffia branches and threw some cowry shells gently in front of her. Chief Sombo sat next to her on a wooden stool, looking at her keenly and with great concern. Fenbandu collected the twelve cowry shells from the mat, spoke some incantations on them, and gently threw them down again. She held the tail of a mysterious animal in her left hand and played with the shells with the fingers of her right hand. She looked at Chief Sombo with a contented expression and said, "Although Paramount Chief Memah is busy, he will surely come to grace the graduation ceremony in Ngaingah."

"Really?" questioned Chief Sombo.

"Yes, I can see him in Ngaingah on the day of the graduation," Fenbandu reiterated.

"Also, I can see a crowd of rowdy children heading towards Ngaingah on that important day," she continued. "Chief Sombo, Ngaingah is today enjoying the last of her prosperity. After you, the village will return to dust."

She broke a piece of white kola, gave it to the chief, and they chewed it while chatting convivially about the successful time they had had in Ngaingah that year. She continued playing with the cowry shells and told Chief Sombo that one of the female initiates called Finda was not going to participate in the graduation exhibition in Ngaingah, because she would be suffering from a trifling cold on that day.

"Oh, no," Chief Sombo said with great concern in his eyes. "I would like all the girls to dance in the presence of their families so that everyone can be happy on that day."

"Humm!" Fenbandu said and continued to play with the shells on the mat. Chief Sombo also recited an incantation with open hands, saying "Amee-nah!" after every verse.

"Well, Massar Sombo, it's not going to be anything very serious. Finda can participate if she feels well enough. But I don't see her to be in good health on that day," Fenbandu said.

"Can I make any sacrifices to stop these evil spirits from disturbing Finda on that day?" the chief inquired.

81

"Of course. Take few white and red kola nuts, an egg, and a handful of rice flour and go to the oracle of the Kuyoh Mountain. Give these gifts to the spirits of the dead. God will then answer your prayers."

When Chief Sombo left Fenbandu's hut, another family was waiting to see her. They had come from a distant village called Dandu to consult the psychic about their daughter's marriage and to ensure her fertility. Since the death of Tewah Korfeh, Fenbandu's hut had attracted many visitors who came in a steady stream to consult her.

She traveled to distant villages in the Kissi country and was highly respected. In her hut hung a leopard's skin given to her by Chief Sombo, when he used to go on hunting trips in his youth. There were also many amulets on the walls of her hut, and jugs of different sizes; knives too. Among the cowry shells she threw on the mat during her psychic consultations, there were also dried seeds from strange plants, mixed with beads. She hardly smiled and told her clients the truth. They loved her for that.

Surnah was among those who came to consult Fenbandu during the graduation season. Slim, vivacious, with long black hair that rested on her back, she was the prettiest among the young women in the village, and considered an angel of beauty. But she had suffered many misfortunes in marriage and was not lucky enough to bear a child.

As soon as the family from Dandu had finished its consultation with Fenbandu, Surnah entered, dragging her feet as she had been reluctant to consult a psychic and was only doing so because her many friends in the village had insisted. They felt that Fenbandu would be able to help her. When she entered Fenbandu's hut, the famous psychic felt very sorry for her. Surnah smiled like an innocent child, bowed her head, and played with her toes.

She always looked shy, but Fenbandu encouraged her to speak freely.

"Well, Mama (Grandma) Fenbandu, I don't really know what's happening to me. I can't have children. I really want to have a child, Mama," she pleaded earnestly with teary eyes, continuing to hide her face.

Fenbandu played with her cowry shells and said, "Choire-nuh (my daughter) Surnah, you were not supposed to be in this condition in the first place. God made you to bear as many children as you would like, but your late father had many wives and one of them, a hard-hearted, evil woman who died many years ago bewitched you. She was also responsible for your father's death." Fenbandu told her honestly and with a kindness that made Surnah fix her eyes on the great psychic with astonishment.

Fenbandu shook the cowry shells on the mat again and again, gazing at the shells with a stern countenance. Surnah knew that that wasn't a good sign. Fenbandu disclosed to her that the same evil lady was responsible for the deaths of all of Surnah's infant brothers and sisters.

Surnah was a little girl when her father died of trifling cold and her mother single-handedly assumed the responsibilities of caring for all her many children. It was a great burden for a woman to carry among the Kissi. Surnah had a little brother, Tamba, and a little sister, Yawah. In Fenbandu's hut, she sat sadly and shook her head in complete disbelief. She shed tears, and her face looked pale and angry at the same time. She hated her mother's mate who had done such evil to her father.

Fenbandu looked at Surnah with confident eyes as she continued, "Surnah, I can see your mother's mate in this room. She is telling me to tell you that she is very sorry for all that she did to you and to your father. She has begged me to loosen your womb so that you can bear children. She is under punishment for all the evil she did on Earth. Ah, she has disappeared."

"Mama Fenbandu, are there any sacrifices that I can make?" Surnah asked earnestly.

"Of course, my daughter. Take few kola nuts and tie them in a bundle. Pray on them and throw them in the Ndopie River," Fenbandu said.

She also told Surnah that she needed to bathe with some exotic leaves that she would pick from a small plant in the forest. She was to cook the leaves in a pot and was to bathe with them, and she was also to cook some rice and to give the food to strangers in Ngaingah.

From that day on, Surnah admired and respected Fenbandu. She listened attentively and cried for her late father, remembering the bush meat he used to bring home from his many hunting expeditions. As a girl, she loved to eat it and had missed it greatly over the years.

As soon as she left Fenbandu, she ran to her mother's hut and told her everything. Her mother later told her that her mate was called Tusu, and that she had indeed been a devil in her day. Fenbandu could have told Surnah her name, but Kissi psychics don't like naming people.

After few months, Surnah became pregnant and went to give Fenbandu the good news. She spread the word around the village that Fenbandu was a wonderful psychic.

The day after Surnah's visit to Fenbandu was the long-awaited Sandi exhibition day in Ngaingah. The arrival of Paramount Chief Jabba was announced by the blowing of an elephant tusk. Gunshots echoed intermittently in the village. Crowds of people from other villages poured into Ngaingah. There was wine and food in abundance for since it was an important occasion, a cow had been killed.

Earlier, men had been permitted to enter the Sandi camp where they had built stands for the shaker players to sit on. The young women were nowhere to be found. They were still in the belly of the Sandi god, prevented from having any human interaction. They had participated in many rehearsals over the past weeks in their secret hideouts, and now exhibition day was at hand. Although Paramount Chief Jabba had already entered the village protected by chiefdom police with their batons, his horn blower continued to blow the elephant tusk. Famous shaker players and the best samba drummers were also among his entourage that included the chiefdom counselor, Ketor.

The lodge in Ngaingah was already prepared for him, and the joyous atmosphere in the village was obvious in every quarter, especially around the courthouse. A gust of wind blew huge clouds of dust and debris which engulfed the dancers, but they didn't care. It only added to the significance of the occasion.

The chiefs and elders greeted the paramount chief by removing their hats, and the women removed their head-ties. Most of them bowed in the presence of the paramount chief. The drummers played non-stop. They also eulogized the paramount chief as 'the lion of Ngaingah' and sang songs that lauded the magnitude of his greatest achievements in the Kissi-Kama Chiefdom.

After the important visitors had eaten and rested, Chief Sombo for the first time lay in his hammock, smoked his pipe, and chatted with a small group of the elders of Ngaingah. They joked the evening away. In the midst of all that, he gathered the folds of his country-cloth gown, put them on his shoulders, and roared. All the musicians and singers stopped abruptly. He said, "To everyone gathered here today, you are all welcome to

Ngaingah. I would like to take this opportunity to welcome our most venerable Paramount Chief Memah and his dynamic entourage. Ngaingah is your home. Rest assured that I will give Chief Memah and everyone gathered here all the enjoyment you deserve till the wee hours of the morning. I pray that the spirits of our ancestors and Almighty God will guide and protect us all. Thank you for coming to Ngaingah," Chief Sombo concluded amid a thunderous applause.

Yamba Farangoh, who was sitting silently near the paramount chief, yelled out, calling Chief Sombo 'the gorilla of Kissi-Kama.' There were chuckles from the crowd of merrymakers as they continued to listen attentively. The drummers and singers stopped playing, and the onlookers stood as if nailed in the floor. When the paramount chief was around, no one else spoke, except the griot or an elder. A singer might yell a chorus and the drummers might give a strange beat for silence. At certain times, even dogs couldn't bark, because these people had charms that could prevent noise when an important person was about to speak.

Chief Memah then stood and gathered the huge sleeves of his country-cloth gown and said, "To Chief Sombo and all the chiefs and elders here in Ngaingah today, and to the merrymakers who have come to make this Sandi graduation ceremony a success, and to the people of Kissi-Kama: I would like to tell all of you that I am very proud of you. I am always pleased to come to honor your invitations, especially when it's on this auspicious occasion of the graduation of our young Sandi graduates. Chief Sombo has shown over and over that he is indeed, according to our famous griot, Yamba Farangoh, 'the gorilla of Kissi-Kama.' He has shown great respect for our traditions, and I have admired him

86

exceedingly. Well, not to prolong the occasion, I would like to open the festivities now. Dance till the wee hours of the morning. May God bless all of us."

His horn blower blew the horn for over three minutes, and then there was silence and Yamba Farangoh yelled a few euologies. He called the paramount chief 'the elephant of Kissi-Kama.' The drums thundered and the shaker players raised some choruses. As the moonlight continued to shed its brilliance over the village, the chief and the elders stood and danced to the traditional music. They danced by spreading the huge folds of their country-cloth gowns. The women wiped the faces of the chiefs and elders with their head-ties, and then waved the head-ties gently in front of them to create a cool breeze, and cheered for them. That was how the dancing and festivities commenced in Ngaingah that evening.

Food, wine, and even the local gin was in abundance. There were drunkards sprawled in the remote corners of the village. Some of the villagers threw cold water in their faces to get them to respond. Some stood up in a haggard way and danced sideways, only to fall on the floor again, unconscious. Some didn't wake up till the next day. They slept among the goats that bleated all night long in their ears. They smelt cow dung and dogs barked at them. They were lucky because Ngaingah was particularly clean on that day due to the presence of the paramount chief.

As long as the paramount chief was awake, the singers, elders, and the villagers danced, and no one slept. The horn blower continued his job non-stop. Yamba Farangoh yelled intermittently, and chiefdom police officers kept the peace. The festivities stopped when Paramount Chief Memah retired, though the drumming continued till the early hours of the morning.

The night air blew some cold, wet winds into the village, and dew was visible on the leaves and grass. The brilliance of the moonlight had already faded. Most parents held tightly to their children, since there were many strangers in the village. Not that the Kissi were bothered about child molesters; they were concerned about witches and cannibals.

The start of the Sandi ceremonies was signaled by the chorus of frogs and toads coming from the swamps near Ngaingah. The cocks crowed, and owls and toucans hooted on the distant trees. The paramount chief was still sound asleep, and Chief Sombo made all possible arrangements before he awoke so that the festivities could start before the sun stood too high in the sky. He gathered his elders, and they went to pour libation at the shrine of the Ndopie and to recite some incantations begging the gods for a successful graduation day in Ngaingah.

On their way back to the village, they saw the sun fighting some dark clouds to rise in the far horizons. Butterflies circled around them and then sat gently on their heads. They never killed them, only brushed them away gently, since they considered them the spirits of their forebears. Monkeys cried and jumped rudely and relentlessly on the branches. The villagers never bothered them, although the hunters sometimes killed and ate them. Monkey meat was delicious, the Kissi said.

At the exhibition site, the cleaning had been done. The chiefdom police were already stationed there to discourage naughty boys from disturbing the young graduates who were still hidden from outsiders. The drummers and shakers were still playing and some dancers were still dancing. Everyone was happy in the village. It was the day of the Sandi graduation. It was also the day the Sandi god would release the young women who were hidden in her belly, as it was said by the Kissi. The parents and husbands-to-be felt a special joy because their loved ones were now ready to be united in the bond of marriage. Some village urchins had hidden themselves in the bushes to spy on the graduates or on their sisters whom they had not seen over a couple of months.

Frantic preparations were underway as the time to commence the Sandi ceremony approached. The graduates and dancers were now removed from their secret hideouts but were visible only to the elders. Their faces were painted with the sacred white chalk they had excavated from the swamp near Ngaingah. They wore short skirts made of loose raffia which reached their legs. The Sandi educators or philosophers did everything to make them look pretty. They had beads of different colors around their necks and also around their waists. They sat on a long mat, with bowed heads, not looking at the face of anyone, while dances continued in the village and the horn blower did his job. The entire village was now awake. Even the paramount chief had awakened. Chief Sombo and the elders went and made curtsies which was their traditional way of greeting such an important personage in their midst. The guns echoed, and the drummers played non-stop. As usual when they greeted the paramount chief, the women bowed their heads and removed their head-ties. The paramount chief responded with a contented countenance, and they exchanged pleasantries.

The shaker players drew huge crowds in the village. They had danced to greet Paramount Chief Memah. They stood outdoors and played while the dancers danced. The shaker players then left and went to the initiation camp where the day's dancing was to take place. The paramount chief waved to them, and they nodded, acknowledging his presence respectfully.

The samba player on that day was Komeh himself. When he grew tired, Jimmy, an old man, came to his aid. The shaker players had sat on the long stand that was constructed for them. The chief and the elders entered, and the onlookers cheered for them. One could have spat and the saliva not reach the ground because of the huge crowds that had gathered at the initiation camp. It was highly congested. Just warming up, Komeh pounded the samba, singing tunes of happiness and grace.

The shaker players sang slowly with their lovely voices, as if sparrows were singing on that stand. They sang sweet songs, and the dancers and the onlookers looked on admiringly. They were gifted singers and the best shaker players among the Kissi. There were enormous blasts from the cannons, and the horn blowing continued unabated. The dancing would not begin until Paramount Chief Memah entered the initiation camp with his entourage and indicated with a wave that the program should commence.

It wasn't long before the chiefdom police officers entered and took up their positions. There was thunderous applause, when Chief Sombo appeared. The Paramount Chief Memah was now seated, and Chief Sombo gathered the huge gown he wore and stepped forward majestically. He had been in a cloud of dust, and his sandals were already dirty. He waved, and everything was silent, the atmosphere lively but tense. Chief Sombo told everyone to recognize the presence of Paramount Chief Memah. The paramount chief waved, and the dancing commenced. The chiefdom police officers were on high alert.

Komeh pounded the drum and the shakers answered. It was at this point that the Kissi graduation day song was sung.

The dancing area was neatly surrounded with sticks and palm branches that hid the graduates from the spectators. The huge crowd stood in a semicircle, the shaker and players ensconced on the stand built for them. Komeh and his drummers sat below them. Chief Sombo waved again, and the head of the Sandi dancers, the head philosopher, started the dance. The shaker players yelled, and she responded with an "ah!-yeh!" at the highest pitch. The shakers responded with an urgent beat. The dancer's face was painted white. She had a cow's tail in her right hand and shook it as she danced by, wiggling her buttocks and appearing to break herself into two halves. It was a mysterious dance, and the onlookers stood awestruck as they saw such an incredible wonder. In the dancer's left hand was a white handkerchief. When she approached the place where the paramount chief and the elders sat, she bowed, still dancing, knelt and respectfully handed the white handkerchief to the paramount chief. He stood and embraced her. She made a curtsy, and Komeh responded with some gentler beats. The dancer altered her movements and the drum beats followed suit. She leaned from side to side, nodding her head gently as if preparing to receive gifts from the spectators. The shaker players played and sang graduation songs non-stop with their tuneful voices. The crowd echoed them and made responsive gestures. The shakers shook with even greater vigor.

The dancer who later became known as "Yow-voh" (bird) went to confront Komeh and his samba. She danced energetically to his beats, answering all his calls and the samba beats excellently. She gesticulated with her hands, shook her head, and swiveled her buttocks in a sexy way which the spectators enjoyed. Komeh then played an unusual beat and, still dancing and waving to the crowd, Yow-voh turned away and disappeared behind the thatched wall and secret location from which she had appeared. She was kissed by the other philosophers and graduates who thanked her for opening the dancing for them. They joked and smiled happily. The huge crowd had applauded continuously because she pleased them well. She was among the best dancers in Kissi-Kama Chiefdom. Many gifts were thrown her way, but she couldn't pick them up. Other people picked up gifts for the dancers. They were then divided among them after the celebration.

These were the joyful days in the Kissi-Kama Chiefdom. Such sacred initiation ceremonies and exhibitions brought peace and unity among the Kissi. The sun stood high in the sky and the philosophers kept watchful eyes on it. They hurried to do what was necessary before it set.

Komeh was instructed to play the beats of the graduation day exhibition songs and to invite all the dancers to emerge individually from their hiding places. Since it was the start of the dance, they came in a single file, dancing to greet the paramount chief, the elders, and the spectators. They bowed as they danced, stepping in time with the beating of the drums. When they reached the shakers, they dispersed with some unique footwork. Many gifts were thrown at them, but they continued dancing and smiling, challenging the rhythms of the samba and the shakers. They then returned to their hiding place as the huge crowd roared for more. They rested for a few minutes, waiting to be called out individually.

Another interesting aspect of the Sandi dance was that the dancers improvised footwork on the spur of the moment to suit the rhythm of the shakers and the samba. In their dancing, they imitated their fathers and mothers, women in pain after the tragic death of a son or daughter or some other tragic event, all the while dancing with intricate foot movements.

In those days, the British pound, shillings, and pence were used in colonial Africa. Although the Kissi manufactured their own Kissi penny from iron, they still used the colonial currency as a medium of exchange. The British pound was like a gem in those days, so the dancers smiled when a British pound or a shilling was presented to them.

It was during this dancing that some families looked for wives for their children. They selected the beautiful virgins for their sons to marry. Such families would then participate actively in the dance during the Sandi exhibition ceremony. They even paid the initiation fees for the young women and gave them many gifts. The parents of such lucky women were so delighted that they tied bundles of head-ties on their heads which made them look like Moslem mullahs. They also painted their faces.

The young women who had not been chosen continued to dance although their faces looked pale and sulky. The shaker players tried to cheer them up with witty songs. The elders focused their attention on these disgruntled Sandi dancers and showered gifts on them. At some point, dancers emerged and again bowed at the feet of the elders before the dancing continued. This was to thank them for organizing such a successful graduation day and for their initiation into womanhood.

The shaker players were the most prestigious singers of their time and were renowned in the entire Kissi chiefdom. They could sing for many days with the same pitch, power, and resonance. Many people thought that these wonderful voices were acquired through charms given to the singers by the powerful psychics. Today, they are all dead and gone but remain in the annals and mythology of the Kissi, their songs still so fresh that they are sung even to this day. They helped to preserve the oral tradition and excellent culture which anyone can see today.

The dancing had gone well, and at dusk took a slower pace. This was to help families finish paying the graduation fees. That night, the moon again blessed them and dancing continued in the village until the next day. The paramount chief had retired to the lodge in Ngaingah, but his exhausted horn blower was still blowing the horn. The Sandi dancers were so tired that they retired to the bush hailed as the best dancers in Kissi-Kama.

The next day, in the presence of the paramount chief and the elders, the young women were displayed in the village square. They sat with bowed heads on long mats woven with raffia branches. Their hair was neatly plaited and beads had been hung at the ends of the braids. They looked like innocent and beautiful virgins, ready to go to their husbands. There also the dancing continued. People showered them with gifts, and the girls giggled when Yamba Farangoh yelled witty songs, which sometimes ended in yawning. First, the paramount chief spoke and then Chief Sombo made concluding remarks. That was how the Sandi graduation ended in Ngaingah that year. The relatives and families paid the fees for their children and the elders released them to their care.

For some days, the young Sandi women went around with their pretty faces looking as bright as angels, but they remained silent with serious or business-like expressions.

The dancing moved to individual homes amid the sound of continuous and heavy gunfire.

Unlike the Sandi, the Poro graduation was sometimes held without ceremony. On the day of the graduation, the young men left the Poro bush individually and re-entered the village. They sat on long raffia mats and waited for their parents to pay their graduation fees and for the genie to release them. The paramount chief's horn sounded in the distance. He was returning to his home at Dia with many domestic animals and even some young concubines. Most households returned to thank Chief Sombo and the elders in Ngaingah for organizing such successful Sandi and Poro Society activities. This was how Ngaingah became one of the most thriving economies in Kissi-Kama Chiefdom.

Chapter 12

Hunting in Ngaingah

There was a saying in those days in the Kissi-Kama Chiefdom, that if you wanted to eat bush meat, you had to go to Ngaingah. Rock pythons, like lions, tigers, and leopards, roamed the countryside, and anyone who killed them was considered a deity. To make themselves invincible, the best hunters prepared themselves with amulets and other charms which they got from their psychics and country doctors. With these special charms, some of them could kill elephants single-handedly. Such men became venerable elders among the Kissi but the positions of paramount or village chief could only be inherited through the family lineage.

The Kissi used many methods during their hunting games which took place all year round. One of their methods was called 'vesia womdoh.' This was a way of encircling the shrubs on the outskirts of the village and searching with their bare hands for entrapped animals. As the search progressed, they would move to the center cautiously till they caught the animal. Some cunning animals managed to escape but many were caught.

During the distribution of the carcasses of the animals, it was easy to distinguish latecomers from those who had started the hunt. Those who joined the hunt earlier, touched an object such as a leaf or a plant and kept it a secret until afterwards. When the time came to share the meat, the hunters would ask for those who had touched objects before the hunting commenced. Those suspected of coming late were questioned about what was touched.

If they answered correctly, they got an equal share of the meat. If they did not, they received the smaller portions.

Another method of hunting was called 'dosuleng,' in which the most experienced hunters scouted for the paw prints of animals in the forest. When they found them, they came to Ngaingah, informed the others, and then led a hunting expedition to chase the animals. Only highly gifted hunters went on such expeditions, because they sometimes encountered lions, tigers, and elephants which were considered dangerous. They also sometimes saw the very angry and dangerous bush hogs. The hunters called an elephant a 'moving mountain' but soon realized that although these animals were huge, they ran like cars in the forest. Sometimes the chases took a few days before the animals were cornered.

Still another method was 'dosuleng a-tun-dah,' which involved sending special tracking dogs to smell the fresh prints of bush animals. The dogs would then lead the hunters to the animals. The Kissi also used special charms to lure animals from the forests; when they entered the village, they were caught by the hunters. The dogs sometimes caught the smaller animals, but they only barked at lions, tigers, and elephants until the hunters arrived.

There was another method called 'Nya-ngor-leng' which was done by both hunters and boys in Ngaingah. They kept snares in the forest to catch nocturnal animals, as well those active during the day. These deadly snares were set all over the forest and their location was indicated by marking selected trees so that other hunters were not entrapped in them. People searching for edibles in the forest were always on the lookout for snares in order to avoid accidents. They knew who had placed the snares and informed them if they had caught any animals.

Hunting was one of Chief Sombo's favorite pastimes, and he was one of those who went hunting alone in the forest on the outskirts of Ngaingah. Do so was a method under 'dosuleng.' The hunter was then called 'dosunoh.' He used to leave the village surreptitiously when everyone was still asleep to go on such expeditions. He would go as far as the Kuyoh Mountain, where it was believed that the most dangerous animals roamed, taking enough gunpowder and a long sword left to him by his late father who had fought ethnic wars with it many years before. The countryside now abounded in deer, bush hogs, impalas, monkeys, and pythons with a few elephants and other wild animals in more distant forests. It was during such a hunting expedition in his youth that Chief Sombo killed a bulky rock python. Hungry pythons usually climb on trees to look to far distances for their prey. When they find them they hurriedly unwrap themselves and give chase. When they catch the prey, they wrap themselves around it and squeeze it with their deadly muscles till they break its bones. They then swallow it whole. Sombo confronted the python. They wrestled, and he killed it.

When he returned to Ngaingah and informed the villagers, his kinsmen wouldn't believe his story until they accompanied him to the spot and saw the dead reptile. They were greatly astounded and marveled at his strength. In those days, hunters had special carbide lights tied to their heads. If they shook their heads, the light became brighter and brighter. Chief Sombo explained to the villagers that he had met the rock python wrapped around a tree. He shook his lamp and blinded the reptile's red eyes which made it angry. The python had then unwrapped itself to chase him. Chief Sombo was one of the hunters who had special charms and techniques for killing the pythons. They would grab the tail of the reptile and slit its belly with a knife, for, according to the Kissi, if a snake was wounded, that was the end of its life. Chief Sombo had done the same to this reptile. The python fought strenuously and furiously and died slowly. It stretched itself, snatching at anything in its path, while Chief Sombo just stood there and smiled. He had conquered it.

Knowing that pythons have a massive amount of flesh that tastes just like fish, the people of Ngaingah ate them. They considered python meat delicious. Not all hunters went after pythons, however, for they were considered sacred in the Kissi culture. The Kissi also had a proverb saying, "a fool doesn't hunt a python or he will soon be swallowed by the reptile.' Pythons were usually spotted in anthills where they waited for smaller prey like squirrels, bush rats, and rabbits. If one was spotted at a specific location, the special hunters were called to hunt the reptile down. There was sometimes a furious battle before the reptile was finally killed. Afterwards, they cut the carcass into smaller bits with the knives they carried and took them to the village to eat, tied in broad leaves with ropes they cut from the stems of trees. The little children feared 'kevoh' (snake) and would have cried relentlessly if the hunters had approached the village with such a fearsome reptile. That is why they first cut it into bits. Special sacrifices had to be made when such animals or reptiles were killed in the Kissi culture, so such meat was then carried to the chief's courthouse. The chief recited special incantations on them before the meat was consumed.

Lavalie was one of Chief Sombo's childhood friends. Both of them had gone on many hunting expeditions together, but they also sometimes went on their own. Lavalie had killed many animals before and brought home impalas, bush hogs, and many others, but one night, he went on a dangerous hunting expedition and never returned. Chief Sombo often told this story, even in his old age, and shed tears as he narrated it. It happened many years ago in Ngaingah.

The villagers could hear the echo of gunshots in the distance when their gifted hunters went on such hunting expeditions. Yet one day, when dawn came, Lavalie was nowhere to be found. His family was frightened. That was not his habit. They contacted his youthful friend, Chief Sombo, and a frantic search party went all the way to the forest with their tracking dogs. The dogs were able to track Lavalie farther away on the Kuyoh Mountain. The able, energetic, and resourceful hunters followed the barking of the tracking dogs.

On their way to the forest, Chief Sombo, with youthful energy, hit his left leg many times on the exposed rocks on the footpath. Since that was a bad omen, he stopped and shook his head, telling his friends that they were going on a futile chase; he doubted that Lavalie was alive. All of them stopped in their tracks, greatly concerned. The owls and the toucans hooted noisily on distant branches, and the hunters knew exactly what that meant. Those strange hoots were the dirges of the dead.

As they continued on the same footpath, they also saw a bulky viper that swiftly crossed the footpath ahead of them and disappeared in the shrubs. That was the last sign of the sadness they were to see when they continued along the footpath. They soon noticed that the dogs were barking continuously in one spot. The hunters also saw some evidence of a struggle and blood along the footpath. Most of the grass was uprooted. Then, just a few yards ahead of them, they saw a boa constrictor lying in a lackadaisical way with a bulging stomach. These reptiles had a tendency to appear weak after they have swallowed a large meal, and as soon as the hunters spotted it, they knew exactly what had happened.

As the boa constrictor looked at them helplessly with fiery red, baleful eyes, the hunters held its tail and Chief Sombo plunged a sharp knife into its belly and burst it. What fell out was an incredible sight. It was the corpse of Lavalie, Chief Sombo's friend. The boa had also swallowed other smaller animals which also fell from its stomach. The snake was still alive, but the hunters were more concerned about the dead hunter and started to investigate what had happened. They soon discovered specks of blood on a huge rock where the hunters used to rest when they went hunting in the forest. Lavalie's long sword lay near the rock. They therefore concluded that he was attacked while asleep on the rock. He and the reptile had fought furiously and fiercely until it finally wrapped around him, stretched, broke his bones, and punctured his lungs. Lavalie had died painfully and slowly. The expression on his face showed the great pain he must have suffered. Chief Sombo and his younger colleagues cried like babies on that day, and the memory of it remained etched in his mind. The reptile was buried according to their custom, for such an animal was never consumed.

The hunters then cut a few sticks and some of them carried the corpse of their dead colleague back to Ngaingah. The news of Lavalie's death spread like wildfire in a dry bush. The villagers came together and the tambah (drum) sent a sad message to the distant villages. Finda, Lavalie's concubine, loosened her hair and cried stormily. She fell many times on the muddy ground since the incident took place during the rainy season. Neighbors came to console her.

The episode remained a mystery in Ngaingah. Some people were greatly troubled that a man who was supposedly protected against such accidents should have died instantly and so mysteriously. Finda later explained to Chief Sombo that her late husband did not take his charms the night he went on that fatal hunting expedition. They might have saved his life.

Lavalie was buried in a secret location. His widow later married Hallie, his younger brother in Ngaingah.

The rains had ceased but the movement of the clouds in the sky suggested rainfall. An old woman who had gone to fetch drinking water at the stream near the Ndopie River heard a strange noise in bush. She went quietly to investigate the noise and, to her greatest surprise, spotted a bulky elephant that had abandoned its herd and was munching on a succulent shrub. The woman ran to the village and told Chief Sombo about it. The news alarmed the villagers, because normally only monkeys entered the village. They caused havoc by destroying the vegetables that villagers had planted.

Chief Sombo held an emergency meeting with the elders and hunters, including Sakillah the headhunter, who soon gathered his colleagues and prepared to attack the massive beast. The hunters placed scouts to watch the movements of the elephants. They took their charms, swords, and some bottles of their dry gin along to give them more courage for the battle ahead. The hunters encamped on the opposite bank of the Ndopie, then, not realizing that elephants don't need bridges to cross rivers, they hurriedly removed the improvised bridge made of sticks and crossed the river again by a canoe.

They did not bring tracking dogs since they wanted to take the elephants unaware. They remained very quiet and communicated by whistling because they knew how savage elephants became when angry. They spotted the biggest of the beasts which looked like a small wagon. Its massive strength would damage anything in its way.

One problem they had was with the type of gun they used. A hunter had to get close to shoot, for at any considerable distance, the gunpowder didn't reach its target successfully or it was ineffective. They devised a beautiful plan of attack which would show the power of the Kissi mysticism. All the hunters, except Sakillah, would fire from behind the elephants. Sakillah, the head hunter, would stand in front of the elephants and shoot them in the face, and then disappear instantly, as would the other hunters. First, Sakillah crushed some sacred herbs and, reciting incantations, rubbed the substance over their faces. He also applied a white chalk that Fenbandu had given him. After shooting the elephants, the hunters would all disappear. News reached other villages and their hunters had come to join the elephant hunt. They had inserted enough gunpowder into their guns and were now ready to bring down the heaviest of all land beasts.

The plan worked so well that the beasts realized that they were facing a life-and-death situation. Furious, they uprooted all the small trees in the surrounding area and stomped their feet on the muddy ground. The gunshots echoed as far away as the mountains of Njawee, Ngopie, and Mambah.

Kpakah, another hunter with mystical powers, stood before one of the elephants, shot it fatally on the forehead, and disappeared. The other elephants now went on a dangerous spree of vengeance. Zakah, another mystical hunter, came forward and shot another elephant fatally. The bullet entered its huge ear. The elephant staggered, shaking its massive head from side to side. Two of the beasts had received terrible injuries on their bodies. For a moment one of them swayed on its shaky legs, and then crashed to the ground, unconscious. Another one had been leaning against a big tree. As he fell, the tree shook heavily and its dried leaves and dead branches drifted to the ground. Its gourd-like fruit scattered all over the place. Some of this debris rested on the backs of the elephant. It grew tired and collapsed on its weak legs, breathing heavily and making a lot of moaning noises. No one could venture near it. Even though the tracking dogs had seen it, all they could do was to keep barking at a distance until the hunters arrived. The wounded elephant tried to stand on its legs, but collapsed again, and the hunters finished it off with their sharp and poisonous spears. It took a couple of hours for it to die finally.

Kendema, another invincible hunter, gave another fatal shot as he had aimed at the elephant's head. That elephant knelt and lay on its stomach. Another one continued to stagger adamantly and event ran a considerable distance. The tracking dogs had to go and find it. Overhead, monkeys shrieked in conflicting choruses and jumped frantically from branch to branch. Small birds and butterflies sat on the backs of the wounded elephants as if comforting them. An owl hooted on a distant branch.

Chief Sombo and the elders stood at a vantage point on the other side of the Ndopie and watched the entire episode as it unfolded. They joked about the hapless elephants that were only fighting for their lives. When it was all over, they crossed the river and, having congratulated the hunters on their bravery, broke kola nuts and shared the pieces in high good humor. The dead beasts were left there for a day. Butterflies and small birds sat on them. Insects came in large numbers too. Their eyes remained wide opened for a while and only closed slowly as the hours went by.

The news of the death of these ferocious beasts evoked squeals of delight from the villagers, for it meant a lot of meat for Ngaingah and the surrounding villagers. The hunters chopped the meat with axes and swords, then took a rest from going on hunting expeditions. The celebration of their achievement continued for many months and to this day, the might and courage of the hunters of Ngaingah is still told in stories. Yet, when these mystical men died, they took with them the incantations and herbs that made them invincible, so these stories are told only in the oral history as myths of the Kissi.

There is another story of a ferocious leopard that roamed around Ngaingah, Mano Sewadu, Sarkpeh, and Njah. At first, the villagers thought it might be a python killing their goats but since it swallowed their prey whole, pythons never left flesh on the bones. The hunters were perplexed, scouted for tracks, and realized that it was a leopard. The hunters gathered again and with their dogs, tracked the animal to a swamp not far from Ngaingah. It entered a cave when it was cornered by Zakah, and there it was killed, leaving only pythons to menace the domestic animals in Ngaingah.

The death of such carnivores was always reported to the paramount chief, who was also given special parts of the meat. A sacred sacrifice was made and libations poured. The women in Ngaingah were not allowed to look at the faces of dead animals like lions, tigers, boa constrictors, and even elephants.

Chapter 13

The Death of Chief Sombo

Chief Sombo now spent most of his days lying feebly inside his old hammock, waiting for the trivial household cases that came up at intervals among neighbors. He was now very old. His hands trembled as he spoke, and he stooped when he walked. He used a cane to support himself when he walked even short distances. He continued to smoke his pipe and blow clouds of smoke towards the ceiling of his courthouse. He kept a snuffbox inside the commodious pockets of his huge country-cloth gown. Chief Sombo's pigtail had grown gray on his soft head and had now fallen on his forehead, like a weak branch on a dried tree. Some said that it was the pigtail that gave him his powers.

He was still handsome in his old age, and spoke softly, but with an audible voice. Tuwoh, Chief Sombo's wife, also suffered greatly from age. She was always beside her husband, leaving the hectic woman's work to be done by the other wives and their children. However, they still participated in all traditional events and exhibitions as usual and with the respect that befitted their cultural beliefs and traditions. The little children still came to Chief Sombo's courthouse and listened to his stories. Among them now were his great grandchildren. They ate with the chief and enjoyed his company, because he told them stories of their long dead heroes, the same stories told from one generation to another.

Most of the work on the farms was now done by the chief's children and kinsmen. Some members of his council were old too. Early each morning, they came and sat at the courthouse, smoked their pipes, and chatted about days gone by in the village. They knew that they had had great successes during their day, due to their strict adherence to sacrifices and respect for the norms of their culture. The sacrifices and prayers they had said at the oracles and shrines had helped them greatly, and they also believed that they were blessed by God and the spirits of their ancestors.

One afternoon when the weather was warm and it was very sunny indeed, little birds and butterflies fluttered around and rested on the branches of the bushes around the village. The little boys went to pick oranges and mangoes on the trees on the outskirts of the village. There was also a big orange tree in the middle of the village, which had been planted many years before, and since no one knew exactly who had planted it, it was now everyone's property. The history of the village suggested that the orange tree was planted by one Yambasu who was also Chief Sombo's great uncle, but he had died before Chief Sombo was born, so none of the villagers had known him in person. The oranges were so succulent that the villagers loved them, and the tree also provided ample shade. During the hot dry season, they sat under it and chatted peacefully. The youths climbed the tree to pick the ripe oranges for themselves and their elders. They packed the oranges in nets and later shared them.

Tandanpoli's son, Chokah, was an obnoxious urchin who was always in trouble for bullying smaller boys. Even when he had not climbed the orange tree himself, he would keep all the ripe fruits and give the green ones to the boys who had picked the oranges with their bare hands and had been bitten all over their bodies by the red and black ants. If the boys objected, he would confront them with his fists and challenge them to wrestling

107

contests, which they knew he would win, because he was the strongest among them. Sahr, Tamba, Fayia, and the other boys in Ngaingah were all afraid of him.

One day, Tamba, Fayia, and Chokah went to pick some of the oranges. Chokah, as usual, did not climb the orange tree but stood under it to catch the oranges dropped by his friends. He decided to collect all the ripe oranges and give his friends the green ones. This time the boys revolted, but because Chokah was bigger and stronger, he started to slap and kick them. The boys cried and reported the incident to their parents. Korfeh, Tamba's father, grew so furious that he went to Chief Sombo's courthouse to report the matter. Other households joined in the complaint against Chokah who had been bullying their children for a long time.

Wango, Chokah's mother, was summoned to Chief Sombo's courthouse. The chief had already gathered the families that were concerned about Chokah's behavior in Ngaingah. The boys were asked what the matter was. They explained how Chokah had sent them to climb the tall orange tree; the stinging ants had bitten them all over their bodies; and Chokah had seized all the ripe oranges from them and had given them the green ones. The other elders were present and Chief Sombo lay in his hammock and smoked his pipe as they listened to the boys' complaint.

Afterwards, the chief asked for all the oranges to be brought into his chief's court, and the elders distributed them equally in three heaps. Only after the boys had taken their share was Chokah told to take his. The chief then informed Chokah's parents about the numerous complaints his court hade received and cautioned Chokah against any such complaints coming to his court again. The Kissi believed that an obnoxious child should be laid on the bare floor and given some lashes on the buttocks with a rattan to teach him to behave better. Chokah was inviting such a punishment if there was another complaint against him. Satisfied, the families hugged each other and praised Chief Sombo for his wisdom.

It was the rainy season, and the weather became cold at night. In their huts, the people of Ngaingah lit fires that burnt all night long. Chief Sombo now lay like a bundle of wood, his skin too soft and his bones too old to withstand the pressure of his office as village chief. Tuwoh massaged him every night. She had successfully married Yawah, as a younger wife, who would take care of Chief Sombo. Yawah loved Chief Sombo and was delighted to be part of the royal family. She cooked for him and laundered his clothes. One day, as Yawah hurried home from the river where she had been washing Chief Sombo's clothes, the clouds threatened rain, and it poured in such torrents that the villagers saw hailstones falling from the sky. The children ran outdoors, collected the small icy balls from the wet ground, and ate them.

Chief Sombo realized that his last days were drawing nearer and nearer. Tengbeh and the other elders now decided cases in the courthouse, but he was pleased that even in his old age, he had been able to achieve so much for Ngaingah. He believed that as long as the people of Ngaingah continued to pour libations at the oracles of Kuyoh and the shrines at the Ndopie, they would always be blessed with prosperity. This was the reward they would receive from God and from the spirits of their forebears.

The people of Ngaingah went on with their daily activities, but they began to be concerned about the rapid deterioration of Chief Sombo's health. If he were to die, Tengbeh, his next-in-command, and half-brother, would be crowned chief. Although Tengbeh was old too, he was younger that Chief Sombo and still active.

The sad news of Chief Sombo's ill health spread across Kissi-Kama Chiefdom with the speed of a hurricane. Relatives from distant villages started to send messages to the chief's family, telling them to be strong and assuring them that they had their prayers. There was now a steady stream of well-wishers coming to see the ailing chief. Some of them brought domestic animals, tins of oil, kola nuts, and other gifts for the chief's family. They shed tears and prayed on their knees for the chief. The illness had sapped the last of his strength. His eyes were nearly always closed now, and his soft but audible voice was losing power. In his hut, his wives, children, grandchildren, and great grandchildren sat beside him and cried and prayed. When the elders came to join them, Chief Sombo acknowledged their presence with a nod and a faint smile.

Again, Paramount Chief Jabba sent his most trusted emissary and chiefdom counselor, Ketor, to Ngaingah to see what happening and to report back to him about the state of Chief Sombo's health. Ketor went and returned with the report that the signs were not good. Chief Sombo now lay in an unconscious state.

The people of Ngaingah and even the office of the paramount chief started feverish preparations for the grand burial ceremony which would soon take place there. It was the rainy season, and their barns were full to the brim with the rice harvested that year. The women started pounding husk rice and when it was clean, kept it in sacks for cooking during the days of burial ceremony in Ngaingah. The hunters killed bush animals and dried many carcasses. Since Chief Sombo became unconscious, blasting of the guns had started and gunshots echoed all around, announcing that something important was about to take place in Ngaingah.

The clouds threatened day and night, and it rained incessantly with flashes of thunder and lightning. All this rain and thunder had a deep significance in Kissi culture. It meant that a deity was about to die. A gigantic tree that stood on the outskirts of the village fell, knocking down many smaller trees on its path. A few branches fell on Tandanpoli's hut. An owl hooted on a distant tree and a toucan hooted on a palm tree. All these were signs of death in the Kissi culture. The next day, a rainbow arced in the distant horizon and more dark clouds threatened rain. The dogs barked relentlessly night and day, and some of the villagers said this was because dogs could see ghosts.

Tuwoh Sombo had finally acknowledged that Chief Sombo was going to die. She sat on a wooden stool with her cane beside her, crying intermittently as her children consoled her. One night, Chief Sombo's illness took a turn for the worse. He was breathing heavily and showed signs of extreme fatigue, caused by the painful muscular spasms that had seized him all over. Outside, it was windy, cold, and wet. Whispers about the chief's grave condition went from house to house, and the villagers sat sadly indoors, keeping their ears open for any further news coming from Chief Sombo's house. They did not expect any mysterious return to good health on account of the chief's age.

As the sun rose the next day, Chief Sombo's heart slowly stopped beating. At once, there was yelling and great commotion in his hut. His entire family cried like babies, and the neighbors soon joined in. The Tambah (drum) beat solemnly to inform the distant villages of the Chief Sombo's death. The elders, who had gone home to sleep a little, were awakened by the noise and hurriedly returned to Chief Sombo's hut and later to the courthouse to receive mourners. The drummers sang dirges to their mournful beats. Within hours, the sad news of death in Ngaingah had spread like wildfire in a dry bush, and the village was already congested with mourners. Gunshots continued to echo all around as weeping women loosened their hair, or else lay prostrate on the muddy ground. There was crying in every corner of Ngaingah.

Tengbeh called an emergency meeting of the elders and sent a hunter to inform the paramount chief about the death of Chief Sombo. As the mourners poured into Ngaingah, the women started pounding more husk rice in mortars and cleaning it. Every household provided food for the crowds of mourners in the village, and the tappers brought in an abundant supply of palm and bamboo wine.

Chief Tengbeh, as he was now being called, proceeded to the Ndopie shrine with some elders, and they poured libation to the spirits of their dead and made the appropriate sacrifices. They also laid a few kola nuts and some rice flour on the shrine to ensure that the late chief's soul would rest in peace. Amid the buzzing of countless insects, the sweet sounds of birds, and the noises coming from the village, they recited incantations and then returned urgently to the village without looking back.

The late Chief Sombo's corpse lay in state in the courthouse after it had been bathed and wrapped in pieces of newly woven country-cloth. The body was guarded by the chiefdom police who had been dispatched by the paramount chief as soon as he heard the sad news. They were also there to keep the peace and to supervise the frantic preparations going on in Ngaingah. Sitting beside the corpse, Yamba Farangoh yelled some witty proverbs

and called the late chief, 'the elephant of Kissi-Kama.'
Mourners came to pay their last respects.

The people of Ngaingah once again heard the sound
of the elephant tusk on the outskirts of their village. It
signified the entrance of Paramount Chief Memah into
Ngaingah again. The burial ceremony was being graced by
the presence of the supreme commander in Kissi-Kama
Chiefdom. Chief Tengbeh, who was now in charge in
Ngaingah, received these important visitors and mourners,
just as Chief Sombo had done in his day. A large crowd of
mourners went to the footpath to welcome their
paramount chief. He lay in his hammock, being
transported comfortably or 'like a baby,' according to
Yamba Farangoh. He entered Ngaingah majestically and
was greeted by all the elders and more crowds of
mourners. He automatically assumed absolute control
over all matters concerning the burial of the chief.

On that momentous day, the drummers and shakers
who accompanied him played non-stop and better than
they had ever played before. They sang and played in
unison to mark the occasion of an important burial in the
village. Their songs eulogized the late chief for his good
works and for his strict adherence to their cultural
traditions. Rain threatened for a while, but Fenbandu, that
gifted psychic, came outside and stopped it from falling.
Lots of domestic animals were killed and libations poured
in all sacred locations. The elders also went to pour
libation at the oracles of the Kuyoh Mountain.

Chief Sombo was buried in the evening amid
incantations, drumming, dancing, and mournful cries. The
funeral ceremonies continued in the village for many days
and, as usual, many of the mourners sprawled drunkenly
in the remote corners of the village. The paramount chief
returned to Dia and Ngaingah started returning to

normal, but it took a long time for the village to be relieved of its sense of loss.

As the days went by, Fenbandu emerged from her hut. Her face was painted with white clay, and she held the tail of an animal in her right hand. She placed a calabash containing some mysterious substance on her head and, accompanied by some villagers, sprinkled the contents all over Ngaingah by dipping the tail in the calabash. In the Kissi culture, these psychics were always driving evil spirits from the village. Some villagers rushed in front of her and told her to sprinkle the substance on them too.

A few months after Chief Sombo was buried, Chief Tengbeh had a dream in which he saw the late chief who informed him that he was living in a peaceful and beautiful world of spirits. Chief Sombo advised Chief Tengbeh to continue performing their traditional sacrifices and to appease the gods at the shrines and at the oracles, for that was the only way that Ngaingah would continue to prosper. Before he disappeared, he again urged his successor not to neglect this practice.

Chapter 14

Why the Dead Sang in Ngaingah

At first, Chief Tengbeh pleased the villagers well. He followed in the footsteps of late Chief Sombo and his fame went around Kissi-Kama Chiefdom. However, the prosperity Chief Sombo left started dwindling as time passed, because the new elders forgot the shrines and the oracles that they once adored and fed. It was one of their greatest mistakes that would cost the people of Ngaingah dearly.

Chief Tengbeh had had other dreams in which the late Chief Sombo reiterated his advice that he should not abandon the practice of pouring libation at the shrine of the Ndopie and at the Oracle of the Kuyoh, where they also fed the spirits of their forebears. Chief Tengbeh never paid any attention to the advice that the late chief had given him. Instead, he did things his own way, and the unity and prosperity that the people of Ngaingah had enjoyed in the past was now doomed. Chief Tengbeh ignored all the traditional associations that gave rise to public exhibitions, and Ngaingah, which used to be the hub of activity for the Poro and Sandi Societies, now began sending its young men and girls to attend camps in distant villages.

Chief Tengbeh also forgot to visit the sacred places. The shrines and the oracles which, in the days of the late Chief Sombo, had been kept so clean, now became bushy and neglected. In the days of Chief Sombo, even the footpaths leading to the sacred places were brushed with long swords. The chief and elders had made sacrifices there and poured libations to their dead. They had also fed them so well that the ancestors were happy.

A heavy drinker, Chief Tengbeh was neither vigilant nor bold. Instead of trying to raise the economy of the village, he just lay in the hammock in the courthouse, smoking his pipe. He now depended on taxes, so that the villagers had to give him tins of gold, sacks of cleaned rice, fowls, and domestic animals. No children ever came to him to hear stories, because they soon discovered that he was always drunk. They joked and giggled at the sight of their drunken chief.

It wasn't long before Fenbandu had her own dream. She saw an angry Chief Sombo who told her that he wasn't happy about the way Chief Tengbeh was handling the affairs of Ngaingah. The late chief complained that there were no longer any cultural programs and that Ngaingah had totally ignored the feeding of their dead with sacrifices. He added that since his death, Ngaingah had become the least recognized village in Kissi-Kama Chiefdom. The late chief then said that if things did not improve, he was going to do something about it. It was a challenge from the dead to the living, but what action he going to take remained a mystery.

The next day, Fenbandu summoned Chief Tengbeh and all the elders to the courthouse to tell them about her dream. She stressed the point that the late chief had threatened that if things did not improve, he was going to take action to correct the situation in Ngaingah. She also told the elders that she had seen faces of many who had died in Ngaingah and was afraid that they were also angry with them. It was only then that Chief Tengbeh told them about his own dreams in which he had seen the late Chief Sombo. The elders were angry with him for not telling them about all these dreams, saying that it would a good

116

thing for them to start respecting their customs again as a community, even though individual families were still doing so.

Early the nest day, Fenbandu put on her sacred dress which she wore only during important occasions in the village such as burials and public exhibitions. She also painted her face with the mystical powder and carried the tail of an animal in one hand and a calabash on her head. She ran from hut to hut till she had sprinkled the mysterious contents of the calabash all over the village. The cocks crowed. The dogs barked. A distant owl hooted on the branch of a tree and some toucans hooted on distant palm trees, all bad omens in Ngaingah.

Fenbandu urged her kinsmen to respect their customs again. She also encouraged them to make sacrifices at the shrines and oracles on the outskirts of the village, crying out loudly, "Oh! Ngaingah! Oh! People of Ngaingah! Listen to me. Our village is going to suffer some hideous calamity if we continue to forget our ancient traditions and customs. We have ignored the good ways of our ancestors which brought us so much prosperity. Ngaingah! Wake up! Wake up! Wake up and restore the customs of old. Wake up and feed our forebears as before. I beg you, my people, and people of our once illustrious Ngaingah, let us fight to restore our old Ngaingah." She went to the remotest parts of the village, crying out those words over and over again, yet the people of Ngaingah turned deaf ears.

Sometimes, naked from her breasts to her shoulders, Fenbandu came out early in the mornings to cry to the people of Ngaingah. The toads and frogs echoed her cries with noisy choruses in the distant swamps. She told the villagers the truth and nothing but the truth. At other times, she played the role of a village protector and holding a long sword in her right hand, confronted what she described as warriors or witches who had come to invade Ngaingah. She once fought off hundreds of these invisible men and women who, she said, had come to feed on the babies of Ngaingah. She would stab at them, and the villagers saw fresh blood dripping from her sword. The villagers couldn't see the witches and there was no wailing or commotion, yet Fenbandu always seemed to win these wars.

Finally, Chief Tengbeh became alarmed by the number of mysterious dreams being experienced in Ngaingah. He called the other elders to an emergency meeting at the courthouse and invited Fenbandu. They agreed to start holding the same cultural exhibitions as before and also to visit the shrines and the oracles, but that lasted only a short time.

In the trance caused by his heavy drinking sprees, Chief Tengbeh again lost interest. Again he and the elders neglected all the traditional practices and, in disgust, Fenbandu completely avoided them. She cursed them, calling them lazy fools and drunkards who cared nothing for the welfare of their own people or the reputation of the village.

Now ignoring the chief and the elders of Ngaingah, visitors to Ngaingah went directly to Fenbandu, so it was she who received all the presents that would normally be given to the chief and the elders for the village. It made her the richest woman in Kissi-Kama.

A woman called Sia Kolloh and her husband, Nyuma, left Sondokollor village, and came to Ngaingah to ask Fenbandu to take her to the shrine of the Ndopie where she hoped to make sacrifices so that she could bear a child. They brought with them a cock, a bag of rice, and a bunch of kola nuts. They entered in Fenbandu's hut, and she told Sia to sit on a stool while she sat on a mat and threw her cowry shells. She moved them around with her fingers and also brushed them with an animal tail held in her left hand. As Sia Kolloh prayed fervently for Fenbandu to be able to assist her to bear a child, the psychic recited incantations over the shells. She told Sia Kolloh that she would surely bear a child but that she needed to be bathed at the Ndopie shrine.

On their way to the shrine, Sia Kolloh felt confused, for she couldn't locate it in that dirty and bushy place. All she could see were old kola nuts and few old morsels of white powder abandoned there over the years. She remembered the day when her mother took her to see Chief Sombo and they had gone to the shrine. "The place was so clean that someone could have sat on the ground and eaten food there," she told Fenbandu.

Fenbandu then told her that Chief Tengbeh and the elders in Ngaingah were not like the late Chief Sombo; that all they did was lie down in hammocks all day long, drinking the 'Tamba Nanjah' and palm wine. They never bothered to clean the bush paths and never bothered to clean these highly mystical and respected places that served to promote spirituality in Ngaingah.

They reached the shrine of the Ndopie, and Fenbandu asked Sia to take off all her clothes. As Sia Kolloh complied, Fenbandu killed the cock and let the blood drip in the stagnant waters at the shrine. She then prayed to God, recited an incantation to her ancestors, and told Sia Kolloh to sit on the half-submerged rock and put her face in the water. Fenbandu then submerged the tail in her hand in a liquid in the calabash and bathed Sia Kolloh's body. She then drove away all evil spirits haunting Sia Kolloh and gave her the power to bear children. Fenbandu gave Sia a small bottle of ointment which she was to take home with her and apply the contents frequently. Within a few months, Sia Kolloh sent a message to Fenbandu that she 'had not seen her moon.'

Fenbandu continued to have fearful dreams and to warn the people of Ngaingah about the calamity that the late Chief Sombo had said would soon befall the village. But under the influence of the chief and elders, the villagers paid no attention, even when the last rains stopped so abruptly and they could not plant crops in their gardens.

Then one night, strange things started happening in Ngaingah. Countless insects sang noisy choruses. Cats mewed continuously. Dogs barked non-stop, and winds blew the thatched roofs off the mud huts. Another big kola nut tree on the outskirts of Ngaingah fell backwards toward the village, only sparing Korfeh's hut by an inch.

As the atmosphere grew worse, some of the villagers asked Fenbandu what they should do. She said she had told them that they needed to feed the spirits of their dead at the shrines and the oracles of old, but that they had ignored all her warnings and now the ancestors were angry. Just before sunrise, fierce winds began to blow all over in the village. They blew the head-ties off the heads of women outdoors. Even the men couldn't control their caps. The winds were followed by dust storms that covered everything in their path till there was dust all over the village. The birds sang slowly on the trees. Hundreds of butterflies fluttered around and rested on anything they could find. Dogs continued to bark and cats to mew. Owls and toucans hooted in the distant trees.

Sunshine brightened the village in an unusual way, and the people of Ngaingah saw the arc of a rainbow in the distance. They were astounded, for they had never seen such a thing in their lives, nor had they ever seen the sun so bright. The few domestic animals remaining in the village were behaving as if they had seen ghosts invisible to human eyes. The sun seemed motionless, and the villagers were so baffled that they were speechless.

Fenbandu came outdoors and said, "I warned you people many times of the calamity that has befallen us today. You never paid any attention."

She waved the animal tail in her right hand and the dust storm calmed down for a while but then, to their astonishment, the people of Ngaingah heard a mysterious dirge coming from bushes under a kola nut tree which stood near the footpath leading to the Ndopie shrine. The voices were human, but the singers invisible.

Ngaingah oh! Ngaingah
Ngaingah you don't feed us
We've gone to Kuyoh.

Ngaingah oh! Ngaingah
Ngaingah you don't feed us
We've gone to Kuyoh.

Ngaingah oh! Ngaingah
Ngaingah you don't feed us
We've gone to Kuyoh.
(Repeat)

This dirge was sung over and over, and the dumbfounded people of Ngaingah stood transfixed with amazement and fear. As the invisible people continued to sing their mysterious song, in the distance the villagers saw ghostlike figures of all ages with bundles on their heads and accompanied by many domestic animals. They moved toward the Kuyoh Mountain and entered it through crevices. These were the ghosts of men and women who had died many years ago in the village. They recognized Chief Sombo who stood tall in front of them with his pigtail erect and coiled toward his forehead. The dead sang to ask the living to feed them.

The frightened people of Ngaingah stood with their mouths agape.

"How can anyone believe what we are seeing today, Chief Tengbeh?" asked Tuwoh Sombo, trembling. "Fenbandu warned us over and over again, but no one paid attention to her."

The mysterious figures entered the Kuyoh Mountain and disappeared from sight, leaving traces on the hard rocks which are still visible today.

The news of the invisible people singing in Ngaingah spread rapidly all over Kissiland and even to the capital city, Freetown, and to Guinea and Liberia. Many people traveled to Ngaingah to see for themselves where the ghosts had entered the mountain. They saw their footprints and the marks they had left. It was one of the greatest mysteries of the twentieth century and even now, the Kissi cannot explain what happened that day in Ngaingah.

As soon as the invisible people disappeared, strong winds again blew across the land, and the people of Ngaingah discovered that since they had neglected to feed them, their ancestors were tired of giving them any assistance or guiding them towards prosperity. The ghosts took domestic animals with them and before long, the rest of the domestic animals died mysteriously. Eventually, only cats and dogs were left in Ngaingah. The prosperity once enjoyed by the people evaporated as all their crops perished, and they couldn't even produce enough food to feed themselves. For many years they lived in abject poverty, having to beg for food from the neighboring villages.

THE END

Vocabulary

Some Kissi words in the story interpreted in English

Al-jeneh – heaven
Ah!-Yeh! – a joyful yell of a Kissi dancer

Balika Tao-tao – thank you so much
Belan-belan-do – a toucan
Bolah – distant relatives who come to join the fun and merriment at a relative's occasion
Buedu – headquarters of the Kissi-Tongui Chiefdom in Sierra Leone

Choire-e-pae-yah – mystic leaves used to bury the first child in a Kissi family
Choire-nuh – my daughter
Dakah River – a river in the Kissi Chiefdom in Sierra Leone

Dia – headquarters of the Kissi-Kama Chiefdom in Sierra Leone
Diomu-nuh – mate (feminine)
Dosuleng – hunting
Dosunoh – hunter (singular)
Dosuah – hunters (plural)
Duduleng – hide-and-seek game played by Kissi boys especially in moonlight in a town or
E-cho-nang – I am here./I am present.
EEh! – a general cry of praise among the Kissi during public exhibitions or on farms

Fellor – large fan used to winnow grains after they are pulverized in mortar and pestle

Fenbandu – lasting life
Foya Kama – an important town in the Kissi Chiefdom in Liberia

Gbekedou – an important town in the Kissi chiefdom in Guinea

Hae-ya-o-koh – winnow (grains) on my back
Hei-neng-gbeh – lie down calmly/a renowned Kissi psychic and country doctor. She lived in Fosonkodu village and died long ago. She was also considered a deity among her people.

Kaelondon – an improvised balafon used by Kissi during the bird-scaring season on the farms
Kalan-choire-vah – fathers and mothers/parents
Kailahun – district headquarters in northeast of Sierra Leone, named after Kai Lundo, a great builder among the Mende and Kissi ethnic groups
Keke/Kekeh – father or dad
Kiah-bengon – give me some rice grains
Kissi-Kama – one of the three Kissi chiefdoms in Sierra Leone
Kissi Toli – one of three Kissi chiefdoms in Sierra Leone
Kissi Tongui – one of three Kissi chiefdoms in Sierra Leone
Kongotibo – a famous female shaker player who lived in Yegbadu village during ancient
Kuyoh – a mountain found in the Kissi-Kama Chiefdom in Sierra Leone
Koindu – the most important Kissi trading town, in the Kissi Toli Chiefdom of Sierra Leone

Lamboo-lamboo – a sacred tree used by young Kissi women during that ancient time to request big breasts by dancing under the tree while singing a mysterious song with

Mama – grandma
Mambah – a mountain found in the Kissi chiefdom in Sierra Leone
Massar – chief
Makona River – the river formig the boundary between Sierra Leone, Liberia, and Guinea

Ngalan-ga foe-yoh – a vampire
Ngopie – a mountain found in the Kissi Chiefdom in Sierra Leone
Nanjah – push me
Njawee – a mountain found in the Kissi chiefdom in Sierra Leone
N-ge-dun-dah – let's push them, an idiomatic Kissi expression meaning "let's help to graduate them" (bondo graduates)
Nyomodu – a small village near Koindu in the Kissi Toli Chiefdom of Sierra Leone
Nongoa – a town near the Makona River on the Guinea side
Nya-ngor-leng – a snare

Ouh! Ouh! Ouh! – cries of a griot among the Kissi
Oh! Seah! – a shout of great joy among the Kissi dancers, also during other public exhibitions

Paleh-bondo-leng – the Bondo graduation day
Paleh-woh-leng – dry season

Pendembu – a large town in the heart of the Mende Chiefdom in eastern Sierra Leone
Poh-nuh – my son
Pusooh – an ant hill

Queseo – a praise singer or griot
Que-siohn – Africa stock cube with an unusual smell used in cooking, mostly manufactured in the Republic of Guinea   and eaten extensively by Kissi in Guinea, Sierra Leone, and Liberia
See-yon -yee-yoh – to tie-the-seeds, a game played in the coffee and cacao plantations and sometimes in villages and towns in the Kissi Chiefdom. A group of men sit around
a mound and tie-the-seeds on the mound. Winning is often proclaimed by the seed that knocks other seeds off the mound.
Sokoah – Kissi philosophers (plural)
Sokonoh – a Kissi philosopher (singular)

Tamba Nanjah – cane juice, gin locally manufactured by the Kissi especially in Liberia/Tamba
Tam-baah – a samba tied in a sacred location in a Kissi village. The beats of this samba and inform distant villages about schedules and programs in ancient times.
Tambel-loh – tiger
Tee-tah-toh – a game played by Kissi boys with nails or pointed objects in the muddy ground
Tumandu – a Kissi town found in Guinea
Tunga-tunga – mystic leaves with an unusual smell, used by Kissi to cure sprains instantly

Yalar-ka-nah – lion
Yamba (Yambanoh) – a griot or praise singer

Yelor – viper (snake) mostly found in the Kissi Chiefdom in Sierra Leone

Yendeh-Millimo – a town in the Kissi chiefdom in Guinea

Yun-toh- yan-loh-nah – We don't want to be blamed.

Yow-voh – bird (singular)

Yow-vah – birds (plural)

Printed in the United States
By Bookmasters